Medieval War of Europe a

body, mind, sword

An Anthology of Articles from the *Journal of Asian Martial Arts*

Edited by Michael A. DeMarco, M.A.

Disclaimer

Please note that the authors and publisher of this book are not responsible in any manner whatsoever for any injury that may result from practicing the techniques and/or following the instructions given within. Since the physical activities described herein may be too strenuous in nature for some readers to engage in safely, it is essential that a physician be consulted prior to training.

All Rights Reserved

No part of this publication, including illustrations, may be reproduced or utilized in any form or by any means, electronic or mechanical, including photocopying, recording, or by any information storage and retrieval system (beyond that copying permitted by sections 107 and 108 of the US Copyright Law and except by reviewers for the public press), without written permission from Via Media Publishing Company.

Warning: Any unauthorized act in relation to a copyright work may result in both a civil claim for damages and criminal prosecution.

Copyright © 2015 by
Via Media Publishing Company
941 Calle Mejia #822
Santa Fe, NM 87501 USA
E-mail: md@goviamedia.com

All articles in this anthology were originally published
in the *Journal of Asian Martial Arts*.
Listed according to the table of contents for this anthology:

Pieter, W. (1993)	Volume 2 Number 1	14 pages
Pieter, W. (1993)	Volume 2 Number 4	18 pages
Greer, J. (2000)	Volume 9 Number 2	10 pages
Galas, M (1997)	Volume 6 Number 3	28 pages

Book and cover design by Via Media Publishing Company

Edited by Michael A. DeMarco, M.A.

Cover illustration

Medieval Japanese and European suits of armor

ISBN: 978-1-893765-23-8

www.viamediapublishing.com

contents

iii **Preface**
by Michael DeMarco, M.A.

Author Bio Notes

CHAPTERS

1 European and Japanese Medieval Warriors
by Willy Pieter, Ph.D.

15 Body and Mind in Medieval and
Pre-modern Japanese Martial Arts
by Willy Pieter, Ph.D.

35 Swordsmanship and Esoteric Spirituality:
An Introduction to Gerard Thibault's Academie de l'Espee
by John Michael Greer, B.A.

45 Kindred Spirits:
The Art of the Sword in Germany and Japan
by Matthew Galas, M.A.

77 **Index**

preface

There are simularities and differences between the European and Japanese medieval warrior traditions that reflect the social evolutions within those cultures. Over the years publishing the *Journal of Asian Martial Arts*, we published articles that presented the main themes found in this unique area of comparative studies. The most important of these writings are assembled in this anthology for your convience.

Chapters 1 and 2 are by Dr. Willy Pieter, a leading scholar with a thorough grasp of European and Japanese martial art traditions. His first chapter examines the feudal system and how aspects of social organization helped form the warrior ethic, resulting in a mix of scientific and intuitive elements. In the second chapter Dr. Pieter illustrates how the perception of the human body and mind are culturally different in the East and West. Westerners have a long tradition of dualism, which separates the body and mind, while the Eastern approach has been wholistic. The author discusses scientific and medical histories for insight, particularly Chinese and European influences on Japan.

In the third chapter John Michael Greer presents the esoteric side of a European sword tradition as found in the writings of Dutch fencing master Gerard Thibault (ca. 1574–1627). He notes that Asian and Western combat systems have been understood in sharply different ways over the last century or so. Asian combatives came to be associated with Eastern spiritual traditions and seemed to be very different than any Western combative system. However, this short chapter shows that there is actually much in common.

In the final chapter Matthew Galas compares and contrasts the sword arts in Germany with the classical Japanese martial traditions. The period covered by this inquiry reaches from approximately 1350 until 1600. The focus is on general principles and combat philosophy. The study reveals that German sword techniques were as effective as their counterparts in feudal Japan.

The content in this anthology is usefull for anyone interested in either or both European and Japanese martial art traditions exemplified during their medieval periods. Enjoy reading this special anthology dedicated to two leading warrior traditions.

                                            Michael A. DeMarco
                                            Santa Fe, New Mexico
                                            November 2015

author bio notes

Willy Pieter, Ph.D., is involved in interdisciplinary martial arts research in several countries in Europe, Asia, and North America. He received his doctorate in physical education from the University of Oregon in Eugene. Recently Dr. Pieter was a professor in the Department of Kinesiology, Faculty of Sports Studies, at Masaryk University in the Czech Republic. As a leading scholar in the martial arts field, Dr. Pieter is an author with a lengthy list of publications, and a regular presenter at international conferences.

John Michael Greer, B.A., is an American author and independent scholar with a focus on esoteric studies. He translated *Academy of the Sword* (*Academie de l'Espée*), by Girard Thibault. Originally published in 1630, the book is "the most elaborate manual of swordsmanship ever published in any language, packed with hundreds of clearly described and illustrated techniques." Greer's work sheds light on European sword systems, and indirectly brings a fine source to compare with Asian sword systems.

Matthew Galas, M.A., is an American attorney working at the NATO Headquarters in Mons, Belgium. An avid fencer since 1977, Mr. Galas is proficient in foil, épée, and saber. In addition, he studied the Japanese sword arts of kendo and iaido for five years. Mr. Galas has been studying the fencing manuals of medieval Germany, sword in hand, since 1982. He is currently at work on a book about Johannes Liechtenauer and the fighting arts of medieval Germany.

NOTES

European and Japanese Medieval Warriors

by Willy Pieter, Ph.D.

Medieval Japanese and European suits of armor.

Introduction

Oriental martial arts, particularly Japanese judo and karate, have become very popular in the West. Initially, some forms of Chinese martial arts undoubtedly were practiced exclusively by the Chinese when they started to emigrate to the West in the nineteenth century. Due to the secrecy that surrounded these martial arts, it is impossible to give an accurate account of them. Japanese judo was probably the first Oriental martial art to be openly introduced to the West in the beginning of the 1900's in several countries in Europe and the USA, followed by Okinawan karate (Shuri-te) and an unidentified Chinese martial art in the 1920's in Hawaii (Corcoran and Farkas, 1983; Kim, 1972). From the 1950's onward, a host of different Oriental martial arts were introduced to the West, like Japanese Aikido, Korean Taekwondo, Chinese taijiquan and various Japanese and Okinawan forms of karate.

The exact reasons for this popularity of the martial arts are not known. In the beginning, the Westerner might have been attracted to them because of their inherent self-defense potential. At the same time, the strict discipline and self-control in the training sessions in addition to a different underlying philosophical position might have had a certain appeal. Presently, the martial arts are being practiced for a variety of reasons: to improve or maintain one's health, to defend oneself, to meditate, and so on. As mentioned elsewhere (Schmidt, 1986), these martial arts can be considered paths to self-cultivation, which might be yet another reason why they have such an appeal in the West. Some (e.g., Kleinman, 1986) claim that these activities have the potential to break through the Western dualism of body and mind. These authors maintain that people are rebelling against the competitive spirit in the West and its dualistic view of man as consisting of separate entities called body and mind.

The Japanese martial arts, as we know them today, are largely seen as forms of sport that have their roots in centuries-old hand-to-hand combative systems practiced by medieval Japanese warriors. They had their Western counterparts in the European knights of the Middle Ages. As originators of their respective brands of fighting, they share similarities as well as show differences in terms of their philosophical perspective, socio-cultural background, and the influence on modern derivatives of their methods of self-defense.

The European knights and Japanese samurai both emerged and prospered in their respective feudal societies. According to Bloch (1961b), societies separated in space and time have been termed "feudal" with reference to Western (i.e., European) feudalism. It is instructive, therefore, to know how Western feudalism can be characterized. The following features seem pertinent (Bloch, 1961b):

- European feudalism can be seen as the outcome of the violent dissolutions of older societies;
- feudal society is characterized by the supremacy of a specialized warrior class;
- there is restricted social class interaction;
- there is a subject peasantry;
- possession of land is important;
- authority is fragmented, which eventually leads to disorder;
- there is widespread use of the fief;
- survival of the family and the State are emphasized.

While comparing the European with the Japanese feudal society, Bloch observed that one of the differences between them was that the Japanese monarchy would still be the theoretical source of power. The Japanese class distinction was more of a hierarchical nature than the European one, and the Japanese vassalage was more submissive than its European counterpart. The bond of loyalty between lord and vassal in Europe, according to Fairbank et al. (1973), was expressed in more contractual or legal terms, while the relationship between master and servant in Japan had an ethical basis in which moral example and obedience played a large role. This, in turn, is related to the Roman influence and emphasis on law in Europe and, in the case of Japan, the Confucian concept of good government as a matter of moral conduct. Finally, the Japanese warrior would only be permitted to serve one lord as opposed to the European system in which the warrior could be subjected to more than one lord. As far as the Japanese warrior is concerned, however, according to Sansom (1958), this last feature is somewhat contradictory because a warrior who surrendered could become a vassal to a new master. Ideally, this individual should have fought to death, committed suicide, or been killed.

Fairbank et al. (1973) mentions two more differences between European and Japanese feudalism. Contrary to the concept of women in Europe—who were regarded as weak, romantic individuals to be protected and courted—the women in feudal Japan were expected to be as brave and loyal as the men and could also inherit both property and positions in their society. Also, the Japanese warriors showed respect for scholarship and the arts, which is probably related to the Confucian emphasis on writing and learning, although they themselves were often illiterate. A knight, or *chevalier* in French, was somebody who fought on horseback (*cheval* = horse) with full equipment (Bloch, 1961b). A knight would hold a fief for his lord to serve him in an armed fashion. Later, the term came to be applied to not only those who met the above criteria, but who also had undergone a certain ceremony, i.e., the dubbing to knighthood.

The word *samurai* is derived from the verb *samurau orsabjurai*, both meaning "to serve" (Turnbull, 1979). According to Wilson (1982), samurai refers to "those who serve in close attendance to the nobility" (p. 17). At first, the term was only applicable to retainers, but eventually it was applied to the whole warrior class (Dunn, 1982).

The knights and samurai approached their world and existence with a special mental framework based on Christianity and Zen, respectively. It is helpful to analyze their underlying ideology with Van Peursen's (1972) three modes of thought which the author has suggested as a model to study human cultures. This model is meant to indicate some marked transitions in the development of cultures in the course of human history.

VanPeursen distinguishes three phases of thought: the mythical, ontological, and functional modes. The mythical mode is characterized by a certain attitude in which people are thought to be "possessed" by surrounding powers. People are not yet able to distinguish themselves from the environment. In the next phase, the ontological mode of thought, the individual distances himself more from his outside world and asks the question "what is?" In the third phase, participation in and with the surrounding world predominates.

These modes of thought are so-called strategies of culture. A strategy is a set of rules that people, as a group, employ to deal with their surrounding world. It is a way to respond to their environment. The same society can use different strategies over time and different societies can adopt the same strategy or strategies at any one time. In other words, a strategy of culture is a dynamic process, an expression of the way people live in a particular society. The three phases described above are essentially three different dominant strategies that people have employed to cope with their world. The dominance of any one of these strategies implies that aspects of the other two are also present. Van Peursen (1972), therefore, noted that these three stages should not be seen as chronological and progressive stages with one stage following the previous one at a higher level. Instead, the model is meant to help understand the present situation in light of these three stages. By being able to understand the present it is hoped that one can better anticipate a future strategy, although in no way is it Van Peursen's intention to predict the future because this would divert one's attention from present problems and tensions.

In this chapter, an attempt will be made to compare the European knight with the Japanese samurai by first dealing with their respective socio-cultural backgrounds. Next, their education and philosophy will be discussed and, finally, their influence on modern martial sports.

Socio-Cultural Background

The European Middle Ages usually refers to the period from the downfall of the Roman Empire to the beginning of the Renaissance, i.e., from about 1400 to about 1500 (Broekhoff, 1972b; Van Schagen, 1968). It is during this period that the European knights came to the fore. European feudalism started in the midst of this epoch. The countries were in turmoil, partly due to the various invasions that they had to endure (Bloch, 1961a). Europe was attacked from the south by the Moslems; from the east by the Hungarians and from the north by the Scandinavians. It is clear that Europe was left disordered and in chaos.

In Japan, the beginning of the Middle Ages was also the beginning of its feudal period. The Japanese Middle Ages lasted from 1185, when Yoritomo (1147–1199) defeated the Taira family (1160–1185), until the beginning of the Tokugawa Period (1163–1867). These Middle Ages were full of local wars and strife, and it was not until the Tokugawa time that the samurai occupied the top position in the rigid social hierarchy. However, from the start of the Japanese feudal period, Yoritomo established his so-called *bakufu* or tent government, thereby indicating the military origin of his power. In 1192, Yoritomo's bakufu was legitimized by the emperor and Yoritomo was appointed *shogun* (general) (Fairbank et al., 1973). In the two and a half centuries of the Tokugawa time, the shogun adopted a policy of seclusion from the rest of the world. This undoubtedly contributed to the strict social hierarchy mentioned above. For the first time in its history, however, Japan experienced prolonged peace and order.

An eleventh century battle scene depicting an episode of the Holy Roman Empire.

The European knight emerged in France after the tenth century and began to decline during the fourteenth and fifteenth centuries (Broekhoff, 1968; Turnbull, 1985). The rise of the Japanese samurai began in the late twelfth century and lasted until the beginning of Japan's modernization in the mid-nineteenth century although, according to Draeger (1973), the warriors were present in Japanese culture from the ninth century onward.

Education

It is well documented that the knights were thoroughly trained individuals (Broekhoff, 1968; 1972b; Moolenijzer, 1968; Ban Schagen, 1968). That, of course, should come as no surprise, since they always had to be prepared to fight in a war. However, the emphasis on physical training came at the cost of the knight being virtually illiterate. Broekhoff (1972b) observes that the education of the knight was in direct opposition to that of the clergy, who was primarily concerned with the traditional school curriculum. Moolenijzer (1968) also mentions that in addition to his physical training, the knight had to familiarize himself with "the social graces, poetry, religion, music, and dance" (p. 36) although they were not taken too seriously.

Like the knights, the Japanese samurai were prepared to go to war and their education emphasized physical training accordingly. Their physical activities became known as the so-called *bugei* or *bujutsu* (martial arts) (Draeger, 1973). Bu means "martial," "war," while *jutsu* can be translated by "art," "technique." These martial arts were mainly developed and practiced by the warriors though they were certainly not the only ones who either developed or practiced the bujutsu. The monks, for instance, were also well versed in them (Fairbank et al., 1973; Ratti and Westbrook, 1979). The martial arts consisted of both military and naval training (Draeger, 1973). In addition to the mastery of as many armed fighting methods as possible, the samurai also had to learn such skills as the use of signal fires, the building of field fortifications, and strategies and tactics of combat. Although the emphasis was on armed fighting systems, the samurai were additionally very adept at unarmed fighting methods.

For both the knight and the samurai, war was an everyday prospect: they were both first and foremost fighting men (Turnbull, 1985). For both, honor was a central concept in their lives. According to the samurai, however, disgrace could only be undone by ritual suicide (*seppuku* or *harakiri*). To the European knight, such an act was unthinkable, not even in the case of being captured. The knight would instead pay ransom, a practice which did not exist in the society of the samurai.

Philosophical Background

The education of the knight had as its underlying goal the development of the knight's character (Broekhoff, 1968). The same was true for the samurai's education (Draeger, 1973). The difference lies in what Oosten (1978) calls the moral/religious frame of reference of both cultures.

From the Middle Ages onward, Christianity gradually developed into the most important religion in almost all countries of Europe (Oosten, 1978). Its influence on medieval life is well known. Moolenijzer (1968), for instance, relates that the Church valued education of the body as inferior to education of the soul and spirit. Broekhoff (1972b) observes that the principles of loyalty, generosity and courtesy were very compatible with the Christian ideal of a soldier. The influence of the Church is further evidenced in the following three characteristics of the chivalric ideal (DeKeyser, 1975):

- prowess and feudal loyalty;
- the protection of the Christian faith, which was related to the liturgical character of the dubbing to knighthood;
- courtesy and gallantry.

Similar to the knight's code of honor, the samurai had theirs. This unwritten code of honor was called *bushido* (the Way of the warrior) (Nitobe, 1979). It could also be called the Way to die, because it reminded the warrior constantly how he should behave in battle (see Daidoji, 1984 and Yamamoto, 1979). Although the term bushido would not appear in the literature before the Tokugawa time (1603–1868), its formative years were the centuries between 1156 and 1600 (Bellah, 1957). It is true that bushido was a code of death, but underlying this was the loyalty bond between master and servant, between lord and vassal. In other words, the first duty of a warrior was to die for his lord (Sansom, 1958). Bushido in the Japanese Middle Ages was more influenced by Zen as opposed to bushido in the Tokugawa period when Neo-Confucian principles would dominate although Confucianism was important from the beginning (Bellah, 1957). Neo-Confucianism essentially defined the proper behavior in the samurai's social interactions. It was not uncommon that violation of the social etiquette would have to result in the offender's suicide.

The samurai's etiquette was expressed in the so-called five human relationships (Fairbank et at, 1973). These relationships were between ruler and subject, father and son, husband and wife, elder brother and younger brother, and friend and friend. Authority and obedience were at the basis of these relationships and the society at large was regarded as a mirror of the family.

The samurai gentleman, according to Neo-Confucianism, would have to possess the following virtues (Fairbank et at, 1973): inner integrity, righteousness, loyalty, altruism or reciprocity, and human-heartedness.

Relevant to the samurai's perception of his body and his physical training was Zen. As is well known, the samurai were intimately associated with Zen. It taught them indifference to life and death, which was obviously of great significance in a period full of wars. One of the main reasons for the close relationship between Zen and the samurai, according to Suzuki (1973), was Zen's emphasis on intuition rather than intellectual reasoning. Also, Zen taught the samurai that he should think and act as one, i.e., his mind and body should act in unison: no disturbing thoughts should enter his mind which would only inhibit his body's movements. This is clearly in contrast with the view of the Church in the case of the European knights.

Sansom (1958) made a comparison between the European medieval knight and the medieval Japanese warrior in terms of their codes of honor. The differences all seem to be related to the differences between the relationship between the lord and his vassal in Europe and in Japan. This has already been discussed above. Although the bonds of loyalty were different in the two geographical areas, fidelity was paramount to both the European and the Japanese knight. The attitude toward women was definitely different for both. The Japanese counterpart of the European courtesy and gallantry did not exist. This is not to say that the Japanese warrior could not feel sympathetic toward women. To the contrary, the Japanese warrior, too, had to abide by a certain standard of conduct toward women (see e.g., Daidoji, 1984), but it was not comparable to the European case. This different attitude is also evident in the role of women in the Japanese society of that time as alluded to earlier. The last point of comparison made by Sansom was with regard to the taking of prisoners. The European knight would, it is true, occasionally kill his prisoners, but this practice seemed more subject to certain rules than in medieval Japan. It was more customary for the Japanese warrior to kill his prisoners. As far as the paying of ransom is concerned, this was more common in Europe than in Japan. However, a Japanese warrior who captured an enemy of importance could be rewarded for this.

Medieval tournaments served as an area for martial practice and public entertainment.

In terms of Van Peursen's modes of thought, a transitory phase is visible as far as the moral/religious frame of reference of the knights is concerned. On the one hand, they were still close enough to their surrounding world (Bloch, 1961a) to be considered as belonging to the mythical mode of thought. On the other hand, the attitude of the Church toward the body was evidence of the beginning of an ontological phase, in which the individual is distancing him/herself from the world and subject and object become separate entities. This ontological stage becomes more apparent in the later Middle Ages and the ensuing period of the Renaissance.

In contrast, the samurai's frame of reference can be considered mythical: there is no sharp distinction between subject and object (Van Peursen, 1972) or knower and known. This difference has perpetuated in today's martial sports although Japan has certainly entered the functional stage of culture and has learned to objectify the individual: advances by Japanese scientists in medicine and the sciences are testimony to their being able to see a person as consisting of a body and a mind; to distinguish subject and object. Broekhoff (1972a) calls this objectification the reification of the human body.

A technique from the *Gekken Sho* — a combination of kata and applications unique to the Tenshin-ryu, using a special wooden sword for more massive than typically used bokken. These swords are weapons themselves, used in a manner completely different from a live sword or normal bokken. *Drawing courtesy of Robert E. Wolfe, II and Itten Dojo.*

Modern Martial Sports

The medieval tournaments with their formalized set of rules (Moolenijzer, 1968) were very similar to modern day's sport conception (Broekhoff, 1972b). This is contrary to anything the samurai ever developed or knew during their time. According to Broekhoff (1972b), the tournaments and jousts not only contributed to feudal, but also to courtly principles. These latter principles were manifested in the so-called *prudhomme* (courteous, and later, excellent man) and would be of great influence on the education of the European social elite of later times (Broekhoff, 1968) as evidenced by the concept of *gentil homme* (man of good lineage) (Bloch, 1961b) or *galant uomo* (DeKeyser, 1975). One only has to think of the later English gentleman's fair play in sport to realize the farreaching effect of these knightly principles. Examples of activities in modern society colored by the influence of these medieval ideals would be the archery gilds (Renson, 1976), horseback riding, hunting, and the fencing societies (Van Schagen, 1968).

The samurai, too, had their idea of the gentleman. In this case, it was somebody who would adhere to the proper social rules. However, the area upon which the Japanese medieval warriors exercised their greatest impact was the modern martial sports.

The martial arts practiced by the samurai gradually evolved into the socalled-*budo* or martial ways (Draeger, 1975). With the change in the status of the warriors from fighting men to bureaucrats in the Tokugawa Period came a change in their fighting systems. The martial arts that were developed and practiced in Tokugawa Japan are better called martial ways or *budo* (Draeger, 1975). They differed in a number of ways from the bujutsu practiced in medieval Japan. First of all, the warriors were not the main developers and practitioners of the martial ways. Civilians also had an impact in this respect, which made the martial ways potentially accessible to a wider public instead of a selected few. In addition, the budo were aimed at self-perfection rather than killing an opponent, which was the primary concern of adherents of bujutsu. Finally, the medieval warriors had to know as many jutsu forms as possible so that the chances of being confronted with an unknown fighting system on the battlefield—which meant certain death would be reduced. Budo practitioners, on the other hand, learned only one or two do forms. With the development of the budo, the emphasis shifted to development of the self: overcoming oneself instead of the other. To distinguish these activities from their modern counterparts, Draeger (1973; 1975) called them classical bujutsu and classical budo, respectively. Unlike the practitioners of classical bujutsu, classical budo students had to strive to act in unison in order to get to know themselves. So, a shift in emphasis can be discerned from a position in which the practitioner had to act as a whole so as to be able to survive on the battlefield to one in which the individual had to become one with nature in order to self-actualize. The major criterion to distinguish the classical bujutsu and budo from their modern day counterparts is the fact that practitioners of even the classical budo would still be able to kill an opponent. This evolution from classical bujutsu to classical budo took place while Japan was experiencing a transition from a mythical to an ontological mode of thought in the second half of the Tokugawa Period.

The martial arts as we know them today were developed in modern Japan (1868–present). Draeger (1974) calls them the new budo (*shin budo*). Contrary to their predecessors, the shin budo are not primarily practiced for reasons of self-perfection. Individual self-defense, fitness and winning tournaments are now predominant, which goals changed the former martial arts and ways more into martial sports (Pieter and Broekhoff, 1987). Therefore, modern budo, and to a lesser degree modern bujutsu (Draeger, 1974), are more sport-oriented. Rules and regulations set limits to not only the types of techniques to be used, but also to indicate legitimate targets to score points. The emphasis on the sport aspect of these modern disciplines, leading to national, continental and world championships, played a major contributing role in the popularization of these systems. The influence of the samurai is felt in a rather strict discipline during training. Also, the focus is on moving in unity instead of with a disintegrated body and mind although many modern proponents of the former martial ways seem to be more concerned with training the body separately from the mind.

As alluded to above, Japan is presently in the functional phase of culture. This is manifested in its practice of the martial sports as well. The gradual distancing of the subject from the surrounding world, characteristic of the ontological mode, can be seen in Japan's martial training practices: an objectified, scientific approach to training has replaced the more traditional, intuitive way. At present, in the functional stage, another shift has taken place where the aesthetics in the martial sports is being emphasized: the relation, the interaction with the other person, the equipment (such as a traditional weapon, for instance) has become important in practice (Pieter, 1987). The aesthetic value of the martial sports is expressed in the unity of the performer or practitioner and the skill or the unity of the practitioner and the sword and so on. This unity has been termed communication of the heart (Hammitzsch, 1980; Herrigel, 1983) and is reflective of the unity that the Japanese feel exists between life, art, and nature (Herrigel, 1983).

Concluding Remarks

The popularity of Oriental martial sports in the West, especially Japanese martial disciplines, may well be related to their underlying philosophical position. They may be seen as a reaction to a possible negative development of the functional stage of culture in some countries in the West. Van Peursen (1972) called this negative development "operationalism." DeVries (1974) observed that, at present, "the world has been reduced to what can be predicted by a computer" (p. 8). Verbrugh (1974) is of the opinion that compartmentalization, which is inherent in scientific thought, is weakening the intuitive realization that reality is a unified whole. Whatever happens in society is determined by science. All problems are being approached from a scientific point of view and scientific results are applied to explain reality wherever possible. If this is not possible, then the problems are reshaped so they can be solved by the scientific method. Bressan (1987) called this a preoccupation with systematization, which is "a rigid restriction of inquiry to only the systematic scientific approaches [that brings] with it an insistence that all researchers see systems with all phenomena, whether or not those systems are inclusive of all aspects of phenomena..." (p. 123–124). In this view, humans are nothing more than "behavioral mechanisms responding to environmental stimuli" (Spradley, 1989, p. 255).

The Japanese incorporated features from a mythical stage of culture in subsequent ontological and functional periods. Considering the individual as a unity, they employed a holistic approach to teaching the martial sports, for instance. Through physical activities, such as kicking, punching, throwing and various blocking and attacking maneuvers with classical weapons (sword, spear, bow and arrow, and the like), they went beyond sports performance to develop the self. Although the Japanese martial arts, now as martial sports in their modern derivative forms, use rational, objectified methods in their training, the older intuitive approach has not been abandoned. In some martial sports, for example, meditation is an integral part of the training process. "Direct action" in the execution of techniques co-exists with analyses of these techniques according to the scientific method. Competition is also put in a relative perspective: it is viewed as a step toward self-development.

References

Bellah, R. (1957). *Tokugawa religion: The values of pre-industrial Japan*. Glencoe, IL: The Free Press and The Falcon's Wing Press.

Block, M. (1961a). *Feudal society: The growth of ties of dependence. Vol. 1*. London: Routledge and Kegan Paul Ltd.

Block, M. (1961b). *Feudal Society: Social classes and political organization. Vol. 2*. London: Routledge and Kegan Paul Ltd.

Bressan, E. (1987). A preoccupation with systematicity. *Quest*, 39, 2, 122–128.

Broekhoff, J. (1968). Chivalric education in the Middle Ages. *Quest*, 11, 24–31.

Broekhoff, J. (1972a). Physical education and the reification of the human body. *Gymnasion*, IX, 2: 4–11.

Broekhoff, J. (1972b). Physical education, sport and the ideals of chivalry, In B. I. Bennett, Ed., *The history of physical education and sport*. Chicago: The Athletic Institute, pp. 9–31.

Corcoran, J. and Farkas, E. (1983). *Martial arts: Traditions, history, people*. New York: Gallery Books.

Daidoji, Y. (1984). *Budo shoshinshu*. Trans. by W. S. Wilson. Burbank, CA: Ohara Publications.

DeKeyser, C. (1975). *Inleiding in de geschiedenis van het Westerse vormingswezen*.

Antwerpen: Uitgeverij Plantijn NV.

De Vries (1974). Inleiding. In H. S. Verbrugh, *Geneeskunde op dood spoor*. Rotterdam: Lemniscaat, pp. 5–12.

Draeger, D. (1973). *Classical bujutsu*. New York: Weatherhill.

Draeger, D. (1975). *Classical budo*. New York: Weatherhill.

Draeger, D. (1974). *Modern bujutsu and budo*. New York: Weatherhill.

Dunn, C. (1982). *Everyday life in traditional Japan*. Tokyo: Charles E. Tuttle Company.

Fairbank, J., Reischauer, E., and Craig, A. (1973). *East Asia: Tradition and transformation*. London: George Allen & Unwin, Ltd.

Hammitzsch, H. (1980). *Zen in the art of the tea ceremony*. New York: Avon Books.

Herrigel, G. (1983). *Zen in the art of flower arrangement*. London: Routledge and Kegan Paul Ltd.

Kim, J. (1972). *The history of empty-hand combat in the Orient and development of the Oriental martial arts in America*. Unpublished M.A. Thesis, Kent State University.

Kleinman, S. (Ed.). (1986). *Mind and body—East Meets West*. Champaign, IL: Human Kinetics Publishers, Inc.

Moolenijzer, N. (1968). Our legacy from the Middle Ages. *Quest, 11*: 32–43.

Nitobe, I. (1979). *Bushido: The warrior's code*. Burbank, CA: Ohara Publications, Inc.

Oosten, J. (1978). *Religieuze Veranderingen in de Wereldgodsdientsten*. Unpublished manuscript. Leiden: RUL–Institute voor CA en SNWV.

Pieter, W. (1987). Zen aesthetics and human moving. *Journal of Human Movement Studies, 13*, 8: 411–420.

Pieter, W. and Broekhoff, J. (1987). *Reification of the human body in the Japanese martial arts*. Presented at the 30th ICHPER World Congress, University of British Columbia, Vancouver, Canada, June 9–13.

Ratti, O. and Westbrook, A. (1979). *Secrets of the samurai: A survey of the martial arts of feudal Japan*. Rutland, VT: Charles E. Tuttle Company.

Renson, R. (1976). Flemish archery gilds. From defense mechanism to sports institution. In R. Renson, P. De Nayer and M. Ostyn, eds. *The history, the evolution and diffusion of sports and games in different cultures*. Leuven: KU-Department Liehamelijke Opvoeding, pp. 135–146.

Sansom, G. (1958). *A history of Japan to 1334*. Stanford, CA: Stanford University Press.

Schmidt, R. (1986). Japanese martial arts as spiritual education. In S. Kleinman, (Ed.). *Mind and body—East meets West*. Champaign, IL: Human Kinetics Publishers, Inc., pp. 69–74.

Spradley, J. (1989). Historical parallels in science and culture. *American Journal of Physics*, 57, 3: 252–257.

Suzuki, D. (1973). *Zen and Japanese culture*. Princeton, NJ: Princeton University Press.

Turnbull, S. (1979). *The samurai: A military history*. London: Osprey Publishing.

Turnbull, S. (1985). *The book of the medieval knight*. New York: Crown Publishers.

Van Peursen, C. (1972). *Strategie van de cultuur*. Amsterdam: Elsevier.

Van Schagen, K. (1968). Historisch overzicht van de lichamelijke opvoeding 1. Den Haag: Uitgeverij Nijgh and Van Ditmar.

Verbrugh, H. S. (1974). *Geneeskunde op dood spoor*. Rotterdam: Lemniscaat.

Wilson, W. (1982). *Ideals of the samurai*. Burbank, CA: Ohara Publications, Inc.

Yamamoto, T. (1979). *Hagakure*. Translated by W. S. Wilson. New York: Avon Books.

Body and Mind in Medieval and Pre-Modern Japanese Martial Arts

by Willy Pieter, Ph.D.

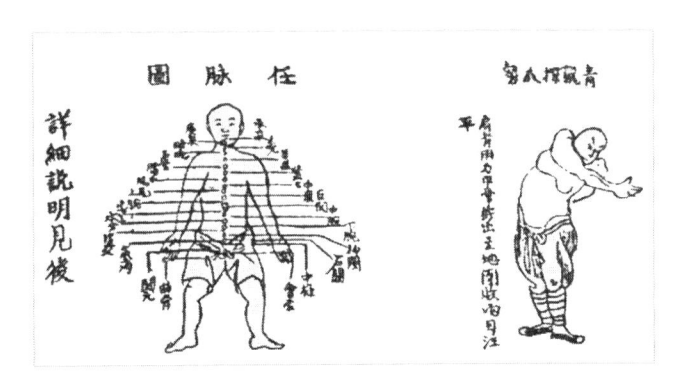

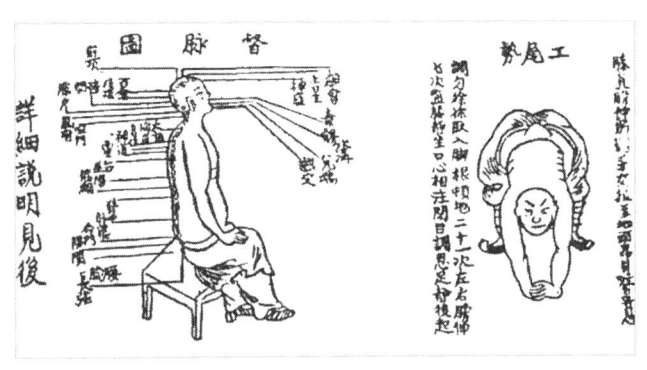

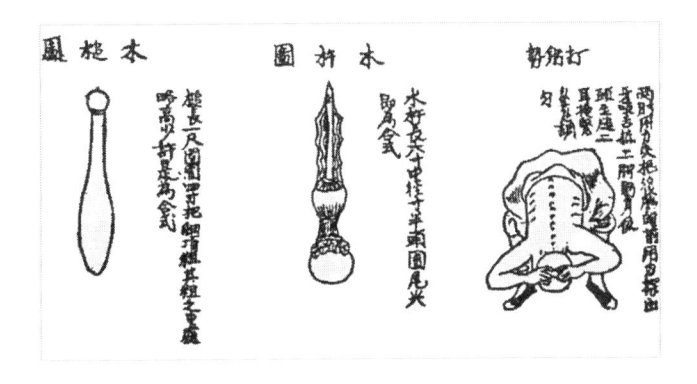

Studying the nervous and circulatory systems is a part
of learning how to "strike the opponent's vital points."
*Photo courtesy of the Government Information Office,
Taiwan, ROC.*

Introduction

The Japanese martial arts in general and some in particular, such as judo and karate, have become very popular in the West. The exact reasons for this phenomenon are not known. Some physical educators (e.g., Kleinman, 1986) claim, that these martial arts have the potential to break through the Western dualism of body and mind. Others (e.g., Schmidt, 1986) have observed that the martial arts can be considered as paths to self-cultivation.

Yet another possibility could be sought in changes that sport and physical education have undergone in the West. Digel (1986), for instance, notices that a shift has taken place in the value system of post-industrialized Western societies. Namely, people are more and more adopting post-materialistic values as opposed to the materialistic values of the era of industrialization. Some of the post-materialistic values mentioned by Digel include creativity, unity of man and nature, and the fulfillment of one's emotional needs. Kurz (1986) indicates that this general trend in Western society is also reflected in the area of sport and physical education where an increasing interest in outdoor activities and "expressive" movement forms—the martial arts, for example—is visible.

This shift in Western values is not only related to the physical activities that people engage in, but is also closely connected to the perception that people have of their bodies. The changing view of Western man from a personalized perspective on the human body as an extension of one's identity to a more reified ("thingified," "objectified") perspective and the consequences of this change for physical education and sport have been described by Broekhoff (1972) for modern Western society. Bennett (1976) shows that a similar development in the objectification of the human body in classical Greek society took place with concomitant changes in physical education and sports of that period.

If the martial arts are held to be an alternative to the present Western dualistic view, it could be because these martial arts are thought to offer a nonreified view of the human body. The purpose of this chapter, therefore, is to explore the metaphysical dimensions of the martial arts as they are practiced in the West—more specifically, the Japanese martial arts—by tracing their development from the fighting systems of the past in medieval and premodern Japan. In addition to discussing philosophical perspectives on martial arts, I will also consider developments in science and medicine that throw some light on the Japanese view of the human body and human movement as expressed in the Japanese martial arts. Since the history of these arts is well known since publications such as those by Draeger (1973; 1975), no attempt has been made to elaborate on it here. Instead, the history of the underlying philosophy of the martial arts will be emphasized.

The Middle Ages

The Japanese Middle Ages started in 1185, when Minamoto Yoritomo (1147–1199) established his military government (*bakufu*) as a separate governmental system from the imperial court in Kyoto, and lasted until 1600, after which the period of pre-modern Japan began. These Middle Ages were characterized by numerous wars between large military families in search of power. Between 1467 and 1568, Japan would even enter the so-called age of the Warring States in which warfare was an everyday occurrence (Fairbank, Reischauer and Craig, 1973).

The martial arts that were practiced at this time were called *bujutsu* (Draeger, 1973). Bu means "martial," "war," while *jutsu* may be translated as "art" or "technique." These martial arts were developed and practiced mainly by the warriors though they were certainly not the only ones who either developed or practiced these arts. The monks, for instance, were also well versed in them (Fairbanks, et al, 1973; Ratti and Westbrook, 1979).

Medieval Japan was mainly influenced by two systems of philosophical thought relevant to the practice of the martial arts: Shinto and Zen. The first of these is indigenous to Japan while the other was imported from China. In the following section, a brief description of the main features of Shinto and Zen will be presented.

Medieval Philosophical Perspective

The word "Shinto" means the "Way of the gods (*kami*)." It has no official scriptures and no organized teachings, and it does not claim any founder (Bunce, 1966). According to Anesaki (1930), the name Shinto was not given to this indigenous religion until the sixth century in order to distinguish it from Buddhism. "Shinto" has more than one meaning (Kitagawa, 1966). It could refer to the magico-religious beliefs and practices of the Japanese, but it could also refer to certain normative principles for ethics and other aspects of individual and community life. Kitagawa himself uses the term to designate the "not too well systematized, indigenous religious tradition of the early Japanese" (p. 22–32). Two characteristics of Shinto mentioned by the author are a fear of evil kami and spirits although life in general was believed to be good and beautiful, so that human beings had to be grateful for their lot.

Secondly, there was an emphasis on purification ceremonies in the form of exorcism and cleaning oneself in a bath to combat evil. There was not much of a concern with moral sins. Rather, evil was seen as a lack of harmony and beauty in both the individual and the group.

Ono (1981) calls Shinto a mixture of ideas, attitudes and ways of doing that are a reflection of both a personal belief in the kami and a communal way of life in harmony with the kami. If kami is translated as "god," it must be understood in the Japanese sense of an object of reverence rather than of worship, according to Bunce (1966). Ono (1981) further relates that the Japanese themselves are not very clear about what the kami are. Basically, kami is an honorific for noble, sacred spirits. Since all beings as well as nonbeings are considered to have such spirits, they can all be regarded as potential kami. However, being an honorific, the term is usually not applied to oneself or one's group. People, then, could be worshipped as kami, but are customarily not called "kami." Kami can be found in the qualities of growth, fertility and production, but also in the wind, thunder, mountains, rivers, some animals and ancestral spirits. Anesaki (1930) observes that "any object or being which evoked a thrill of emotion, whether affectionate or aweinspiring, appealing to the sense of mystery, might be regarded as a kami and accorded due respect" (p. 21). The modern vision of how kami relate to one another reflects the principles of justice, order, and harmony.

"Zen" is the Japanese pronunciation of the Chinese *chan*, an abbreviation of *chan-na* for the Sanskrit *dhyana*, which means "meditation" (Fung, 1983b) or "concentration of mind" (Kitagawa, 1966). According to Chan (1973), Chinese meditation is not to be understood in the Indian sense of concentration of mind. Rather, Chinese meditation deals more with conserving vital energy, breathing properly or reducing desire. Eventually, Chinese meditation came to refer to direct enlightenment and not so much to sitting in meditation or to mental concentration. In Japan, sitting in meditation became one of the methods used to reach sudden enlightenment.

Although the origin of Chan is usually traced back to the historical Buddha and its development in China to Bodhidharma (cir. 460–534), this popular account is historically not very reliable (Chan, 1973; Fung, 1983b; Shih, 1931; Spiessbach, 1992). Fung (1983b) relates that the theory of direct enlightenment as propagated by Chan developed in the so-called Period of Disunity (221–589), a period when China was divided into numerous short-lived dynasties and states. This theory of direct enlightenment subsequently spread during the Tang dynasty (618–907). The history of Chan in China before the monk Hong Ren (601–674) is not very clear (Chan, 1973; Fung, 1983b). After Hong Ren's death, a schism occurred between two of his disciples, Shen Xiu (600 or 605–706) in the north and Hui Neng (638–713) in the south (Chan, 1973; Fung, 1983b). From the ninth century onward, the so-called Southern School became the dominant Chan force in China (Chan, 1973). Preliminary and decisive work for the eventual victory of the Southern School was done by Hui Neng's student Shen Hui (686–760) who, in 734, started to challenge the claim of Shen Xiu as the legitimate heir of Hong Ren (Shih, 1953). Shen Hui's efforts were finally rewarded by the recognition of Hui Neng as the official successor of Hong Ren.

The distinction between the Northern and Southern School is usually attributed to the fact that the former advocated gradual enlightenment while the latter emphasized instantaneous enlightenment (Chan, 1973). This difference in emphasis was only true in general, however, because the Northerners did not rule out the possibility of sudden enlightenment as the Southerners did not rule out gradual enlightenment.

Chan further observes that the differences between the two schools ran deeper than that. Their differing concepts of the mind are at least as important as their view of how enlightenment is attained. Both the Northern and Southern schools believed that enlightenment is identical with the Buddha-nature or the original Buddha-mind (Chan, 1973), which is present in all human beings so that everybody has the potential to become a Buddha. The Northern School taught that this Buddha-mind or pure mind can only be attained by absolute quietue, i.e., after all dichotomous thoughts have been eliminated. In contrast, the Southern School held that the mind cannot be divided into parts with a true or non-dichotomizing mind on the one hand and a dichotomizing or false mind on the other hand. Rather, all activities of the mind are functions of the Buddha-mind and as such are one, as is everything else, because the Buddha-mind is everywhere so that anything can lead to enlightenment at anytime, in anyway and anywhere.

Above: The Peak Flown from Afar—a hill near Hangzhou, China, has nearly four hundred carvings in its slopes and caves facing the Buddhist Lingyin Temple. From this sculpture, it appears that a smile is part of the "Buddha-nature." As Buddhims spread so did philosophic and medical knowledge that influenced the practice of Asian martial arts. *Photo by M. DeMarco*

Zen was influenced by both Buddhism and Daoism when it developed in China during the Tang dynasty (618–907). From Buddhism it took the emphasis on meditation and intuitive insight and it incorporated Daoism's love for nature, its emphasis on the development of one's character and its disdain for a reliance on texts or intellectual discourses based on these texts. Zen would rather stress the oral communication between master and student, rigorous meditation, independence from authority, strict self-discipline and the achievement of enlightenment through an understanding of oneself (Fairbank, et al., 1973). In other words, without relying on any conceptualizations or abstractions, but through direct insight, Zen tries to attain a state in which there is no distinction between subject and object, in which the individual and the environment are not seen in opposition to each other, but rather in unity with one another. Tiwald (1981) calls this a state in which there is no distortion of self, no biased view of oneself.

Zen in Japan

Although Zen was introduced to Japan in the Nara Period (710–781), it was not until after its reintroduction from China in the late twelfth century that it became the dominant religion of medieval Japan (Kitagawa, 1966). In 1191, Eisai (1141–1215) introduced the Rinzai Zen School from China, while Dogen (1200–1253) brought Soto Zen to Japan in 1227, also from China. Eisai and his followers were instrumental in introducing Neo-Confucianism to Japan as well. The Rinzai Zen temples soon functioned as schools for Neo-Confucianism too. Of the two Zen schools, Rinzai Zen was the more influential. It gained the support of the military leaders in medieval Japan and became the state religion of the period. It contributed significantly to the development of art, literature, the tea ceremony (the introduction of which is also credited to Eisai) and the No-drama. The basis of Rinzai Zen was meditation upon *koan*, i.e., paradoxical statements that are meant to train nondichotomous thinking, while Soto Zen emphasized "sitting straight" in meditation "without any effort at achieving enlightenment" (Kitagawa, 1966: 128).

In medieval Japan, Shintoism started to assimilate the main tenets of some Buddhistic theories, and although there was a short time when serious efforts were undertaken to free Shinto from this Buddhistic influence, Shintoism could not help but incorporate a metaphysical basis from Buddhism while its ethics were inspired by Confucianism (Kitagawa, 1966). Shinto's influence on the medieval warrior in Japan was apparent in the ceremonies in which he pledged his loyalty to his lord (Ratti and Westbrook, 1979).

Through this pledge, the warrior became identified with his master to such an extent that he would unconditionally follow him even in death (whether the result of natural causes or battle). This practice became so common (whole families would commit mass suicide) that it had to be prohibited by law.

Zen had a special attraction to the Japanese warriors in the Middle Ages. Warrior leaders turned to Zen monks for advice and they sometimes even retired to Zen monasteries to escape a life full of pressures (Fairbank et al., 1973). Suzuki (1973) relates that Zen had such an appeal to the Japanese warriors because of its emphasis on intuition rather than intellectual reasoning.

Of course, Zen also stressed self-discipline and a strong character, and it also taught the warrior indifference to life and death, which was especially significant in a period rife with wars. Just like his European counterpart, the Japanese medieval warrior had a code of honor. The code of the Japanese medieval warrior was called *bushido* or the "Way of the Warrior." It could also be called the "Way to Die" because it reminded the warrior constantly of how he should behave in battle (see Daidoji, 1984 and Yamamoto, 1979). Although the term "bushido" would not appear in the literature before the Tokugawa time (1603–1868), its formative years were the centuries between 1156 and 1600 (Bellah, 1957). It is true that bushido was a code of death, but underlying this was the bond of loyalty between master and servant, between lord and vassal. In other words, the first duty of a warrior is to die for his lord (Sansom, 1958).

It is clear that bushido in the Japanese Middle Ages was more influenced by Zen than was bushido in the Tokugawa period when Neo-Confucianism principles would dominate, although Confucianism was important through most of Japanese history (Bellah, 1957).

The warrior's contempt for death was also expressed in the custom of ritualistic suicide (*seppuku* or *harakiri*) (Ratti et al., 1979), which was considered to be "the highest manifestation of command over one's own destiny and unflinching courage in the face of death" (p. 92). Although certainly not the only reason, seppuku was widely used to escape capture by the enemy and was in marked contrast with the feudal European custom of allowing oneself to be taken prisoner. Both men and women would engage in this ceremonial suicide. The man would cut his lower abdomen, while the woman would cut her throat. The abdomen was chosen because the Japanese believed that it was there that the soul resided (Seward, 1984). Since the abdomen was the cradle of one's will, thoughts, spirit, anger, enmity, boldness, and so on, it was only appropriate to choose it as the site for suicide. The act therefore was the most symbolic expression of one's convictions and emotions.

It is not surprising, then, that Zen played a major role in medieval Japan, even to the extent that it could be considered the de facto state religion (Kitagawa, 1966), although Shinto held that title officially (Sansom, 1961). Zen monks were not only shogunal advisers, but were also used as intermediaries between Ming China (1368–1662) and Japan. In addition, they were the leading scholars, architects and artists in Japan at that time. In short, the influence of Zen was such that medieval Japan of especially the Ashikaga period could be said to have a Zen culture (Fairbank et al., 1973).

The influence of Zen on Japanese art forms has been well documented, be they the martial arts (Herrigel, 1971; Kammer, 1978; Tiwald, 1981), the tea ceremony (Hammitzsch, 1980), flower arrangement (Herrigel, 1983), No-drama (Koizumi, 1986) or painting (e.g., Shute, 1968). Suzuki (1973) has amply described Zen's far-reaching effects on Japanese culture in general.

Watts (1957) observes that all Japanese arts follow the same format in their training in Zen. An account of this may be found in Herrigel's (1971) work on Japanese archery. Elsewhere (Pieter, 1987) it has been shown that Zen's influence can be seen not only in the area of metaphysics, but that Zen's principles also apply to the aesthetic domain. In fact, Zen's metaphysical position is also its aesthetic view. That is, according to Zen, something can only be considered art when there is no separation between subject and object; when the painter is the brush, is the painting; or when the host is the tea, is the kettle, is the guest. Hammitzsch (1980) and Herrigel (1983) call this unity of subject and object in the arts, communicating with the heart. As far as the body-mind concept is concerned, according to Shinto, the environment and the person are not in opposition (Dno, 1981). To the contrary, the world is filled with the blessings of the kami and it is difficult to draw a sharp line between the person and the kami. In theory, human beings may be considered kami although they are not called such until after their death.

From the perspective of Zen, the individual and nature are also one. Though it is recognized that "nature is the world of manyness" and one is facing this world as a subject, the Zen practitioner experiences a close relationship with the environment: there is a little bit of nature in man and there is a little bit of man in nature (Suzuki, 1974). As mentioned earlier, Zen's view of nature has been influenced by Daoism. Consequently, it would be instructive to look at the Daoist perspective on nature.

Underlying the many things in the world is a Unity called *Dao* (Munro, 1982). It is often described as "nothingness," Non-Being or *wu* to indicate that it has no qualities such as good or bad, large or small, positive or negative, and so on. Dao, therefore, is beyond dichotomization. Dao, however, can be found in individual beings or things. As such, it is called *de*, the life principle that gives these beings and things their characteristics. Through this de everything is linked with Dao, the unitary principle. Although the Daoist recognizes that there are individual differences, these differences are considered ephemeral. One should instead concentrate on the Dao within oneself.

As the all-embracing principle, Dao "exists by and through itself" (Fung, 1983a: 223) and is manifested in everything by means of *de* (or *toku* in Japanese). De is usually translated as "virtue," although Fung, in many cases, would rather translate it as "efficacy" or "power" inherent in something or someone (a more detailed analysis of the word was given by Boodberg [1953] and will be discussed below). Mathews (1975) translated it as, among other things, "moral excellence," while Nelson (1963) rendered it as "power to command respect." This respect is supposedly based on "goodness," on "moral behavior." Tiwald (1981) and Watts (1957) preferred to call it "spontaneous virtue" to indicate its relationship with Dao, which, just like nature, accomplishes everything spontaneously. This spontaneity is also called "non-activity" or *wu wei* and is characteristic of Zen. It is through "non-activity" that one will come into harmony with Dao (or as the Zen practitioner would say, the Buddha nature) and thus reach enlightenment. The concept of non-activity should not be taken to mean doing nothing. It is probably better to describe as "direct action" by which Humphreys (1960) means doing things without any thoughts or planned results in mind.

Harboring something in mind, according to Zen, is referred to as having a delusive or relative mind (Suzuki, 1973). The mind which does not contain anything is called the absolute or original mind. The delusive mind makes a person stop and reflect so that any fluidity, naturalness or spontaneity is lost. This, of course, would be lethal to the medieval warrior because any hesitation would most certainly mean death in battle or combat. Instead, one should try to act in accordance with the original mind. This mind never stops anywhere and it flows like water to fill every corner of the person. In this way, one can act naturally. The original mind is the Buddha nature or the Dao (in its form of de) in us and it is also called no-mind: a mind with nothing in it, an empty mind, i.e., a non-dichotomizing mind.

Japanese Medicine

The non-objectified view of the human body is also apparent in such disciplines as science and medicine. Japanese science and medicine during the medieval period were under the influence of Chinese developments in these areas (Tuge, 1961). Phenomena in the fields of astronomy, such as the eclipse of the moon or sun, and mathematics were mainly used for fortunetelling. Wooden bits, for instance, were used to calculate and the numbers "3" and "8" were considered to be holy. Developments in medicine reflect the growing trend to objectify the human body as Broekhoff (1972) points out.

As mentioned above, Japanese medicine was under the strong influence of Chinese medicine. The old Chinese believed that one would stay healthy if the two principles yin and yang (usually designating the female and male forces in the world, but probably more accurately representing the dichotomized way in which people consider their relationship to their environment) and the five elements of metal, wood, water, fire and earth were in harmony with each other (Wong and Wu, 1936). The five elements would further correspond to five organs in the body: spleen, kidneys, heart, lungs and liver, which in turn corresponded to the planets, variations in climate, and so on. It is clear that, according to this view, people were part of the surrounding world.

In the Far East, many female patients used a statue the doctors provided for them to indicate the location of ailments. *Photo courtesy of the Johnson–Humerickhouse Museum.*

Despite this personalistic view of man and the world, the Chinese appear to have done some dissections of human cadavers, which would be indicative of a more objectified view of the human body. These dissections, however, did not lead to a more accurate insight into the human anatomy. Remarkable are some of the observations on human physiology concerning the blood circulation in the oldest handbook on medicine in China, the *Internal Classic of Medicine* (Wong and Wu, 1936). Even at this early time, apparently it was thought that the blood was under the control of the heart and that it flowed continuously in a circle! The general trend of Chinese medicine, however, had not yet fully objectified the human body. This was also true for Japanese medicine. Japanese priests, who, like their Chinese counterparts, were also the physicians of the time, were of the opinion that the spirit was governed by the heart, the soul by the liver, the will by the spleen and the intentions by the kidneys (Fujikawa, 1934).

Seemingly in contrast with these philosophical and medical positions in China, and undoubtedly in Japan too, was the existence of breathing and physical exercises and dietary systems designed to lead to a physically healthy life so that one would live longer (the Daoistic objective) or be able to meditate longer (the Buddhistic goal) (Hume, 1940; Wong and Wu, 1936). These practices also suggest a more reified view of the human body developing alongside these traditions.

Exercises specifically developed to improve overall physical conditions are termed "intermediary movements" by Broekhoff (1972) and can be considered characteristic of an objectified view of the human body. Contrary to what had happened in Europe, no support can be found in the metaphysical and medical perspectives of China and Japan of that time to support the assumption that objectification of the human body had indeed occurred.

The non-reified view of the human body is also found in the martial arts in medieval Japan. The various techniques were practiced in so-called martial art forms. A form is a predetermined set of attacks and blocks in various directions against imaginary opponents and simulate actual confrontations in battle or combat. The various skills could not be practiced with a partner because they were designed to kill the enemy. Therefore, they can be termed functional or goal-oriented or natural movements as opposed to the artificial intermediary movements (Broekhoff, 1972).

Pre–Modern Japan

The premodern era of Japan started around 1603 when Tokugawa Ieyasu (1542–1616) became the supreme military commander of Japan. The period from 1603 until the beginning of modern Japan in 1868 is also called the Tokugawa Period. For some two and a half centuries, Japan would experience prolonged peace as a unified nation, which had far-reaching consequences for the existence of the warrior as a fighting man. With the country at peace, the warrior did not need to be constantly prepared to go to war. By holding members of their families hostage and by forcing them to spend time at the court where they had to perform various administrative duties, the government also made sure that the warriors would not revolt.

With the change in the status of the warriors from fighting men to bureaucrats came a change in their fighting systems. The martial arts that were developed and practiced in Tokugawa Japan are more appropriately called martial ways of budo (Draeger, 1975). They differed in a number of ways from the bujutsu practiced in medieval Japan. First of all, the warriors were not the main developers and practitioners of the martial ways. Civilians had an impact as well, which made the martial ways potentially accessible to a wider public instead of a selected few. Also, the budo were aimed at self-perfection rather than killing an opponent, which was the primary goal of adherents of bujutsu. Finally, the medieval warriors had to know as many jutsu forms as possible, so that the chances of being confronted on the battlefield with an unknown fighting system—which would mean certain death—would be reduced. Budo practitioners, on the other hand, learned only one or two do forms.

Philosophical Perspectives

Japan during the Tokugawa period was introduced to Christianity while Neo-Confucianism became the official state religion (Kitagawa, 1966). Christianity was brought to Japan by the Jesuit Francis Xavier (1506–1552) and its initial success was probably also due to the willingness of the Jesuits to use mostly Buddhistic terminology to explain Christianity. Moreover, it gave the Japanese "a sense of social identity and solidarity" (p. 139) in addition to the promise of salvation. Despite this success, however, Christianity was eventually banned and its followers persecuted. When Japan went into seclusion in 1639, the little influence Christianity had came to an end, save for some small groups which went underground to preserve their religion.

Buddhism, under Tokugawa rule, blossomed at first (Kitagawa, 1966). The temples were organized in a hierarchical manner to serve the political ends of the government. Every household was forced to become affiliated with a temple to promote the anti-Christian policy of the government. However, increased corruption among the Buddhists led to a growing resistance to Buddhism. This, in turn, led to a heightened interest in Shinto, especially in the latter part of the Tokugawa regime. Among the factors that contributed to this Shinto revival was its relation with the imperial clan. The movement to restore the power of the emperor was, of course, highly compatible with the renewed interest in Shinto.

Neo-Confucianism was introduced into Japan by Zen monks in the previous period of the Middle Ages (Kitagawa, 1966). The school of Neo-Confucianism that was particularly popular in the Tokugawa time was that of Zhu Xi (1130–1200). In China, Zhu Xi's Neo-Confucianism was also called the "School of Reason" or the "School of Law or Principle" (see Charpio [1978] for a comprehensive treatment of Neo-Confucianism in China and its implications for body movement). Sansom (1963) mentions that rationalism and humanism could characterize Neo-Confucianism in Tokugawa Japan.

Neo-Confucianism's direct impact was felt in the area of human relationships, e.g., it defined the so-called "five human relations" (between father and son, ruler and subject, husband and wife, older and younger brother, and friend and friend), which guided the interaction between people. Filial piety and loyalty lay at the basis of the doctrine of Neo-Confucianism in Japan and had a profound impact on the code of the warriors (Bellah, 1957). The society at large was seen as a reflection of the family.

The nation was represented by the shogun and the family by the father. However, if a father opposed the shogun, his children were expected to follow the latter and desert their father to prove their loyalty to the ruler (Kitagawa, 1966). According to this line of reasoning, filial piety was not in contrast with national loyalty, but rather reinforced it (Bellah, 1957). The influence of Neo-Confucianism on bushido was expressed in the devotion of the samurai to his lord (Bellah, 1957). This devotion was based on a feeling of gratitude toward one's lord, which in turn was rooted in the devotion to one's parents and especially the father. Daidoji (1984) and Yamamoto (1979) mention filial piety as one of the characteristics of a true samurai. No matter how much one served his parents, he would always be in debt to them. Being this grateful would even manifest itself in the willingness to die for one's parents, but one ideally would be even more willing to die for his lord. Dying, according to Bellah (1957), had an almost religious quality in this light.

Related to selfless devotion is an almost ascetic way of life (Bellah, 1957). The warrior was supposed to reduce his food consumption to a minimum and at the same time increase his contribution to his lord to the maximum. Moreover, leading a life of poverty was in accordance with Zen, which also taught the warrior not to be afraid of dying. The last feature of the warrior's code attributable to Neo-Confucianism was the emphasis on learning. Because of this emphasis, most samurai in this period of Japanese history were literate and had some knowledge of the Chinese classics. The aim of learning was the control of others (as in governing) and self-cultivation.

The word *do* in budo is the Japanese pronunciation of the Chinese *Dao*. Contrary to the Chinese, however, the Japanese did not take it to mean an abstract, unnamable Way from which all else developed, but a concrete "way" or "road" to follow in life (Draeger, 1975). This "path" was based on ideal human behavior, steeped in morals, which would not only benefit the practitioner, but which would also elevate the whole of society. Eventually, this ideal behavior would lead to becoming one with nature, which, of course, is an idea based on Zen. A blend of Confucian and Zen influences can be seen in this view of the "way." Since the Zen perspective has already been dealt with above, only Neo-Confucianism will be discussed here. Within the Neo-Confucian stream of thought, several schools can be distinguished (see, e.g., Charpio [1978] for a short discussion of these schools), but the emphasis in this chapter will be on Zhu Xi's interpretation because this system was preferred in Tokugawa Japan.

Tu (1971) gives a concise account of Zhu Xi's concept of man and world. According to Zhu Xi, all individual things are manifestations of the Great Ultimate (c. *taiji*; j. *taikyoku*), which was also used to represent the Dao. The principle (c. *li*; j. *ri*), which is the manifestation of the Great Ultimate, is a complete concretization instead of a partial reflection of the Great Ultimate. Aside from this principle, there is also material force or *qi*, which, together with the principle *li* makes up the reality of each thing or being. In man, li can be found in human nature, while qi can be found in the physical form. In addition, man also has a mind which, it is true, is inseparable from material force, but which has the potential to transform that force "into a kind of moral energy so as to reveal fully the principle of man in daily life" (p. 84). This, however, can only be done when the mind has purified itself through self-cultivation, which again is brought about by learning as was indicated above. In other words, there seems to be a passive principle, human nature, which is waiting to be acted upon by a dynamic mind.

Carpio (1978) gives a general outline of Neo-Confucianism, which seems pertinent here. Its metaphysical position is in accordance with Zhu Xi's. According to this outline, as far as the impact of the supernatural on the individual is concerned, people are considered "creative agents," i.e., they are seen as independent of any supernatural beings and as determining their own behavior. Being unselfish is virtuous behavior and will bring one in harmony with the Original Source. According to Confucianism, all people are born with an evaluating mind (Munro, 1982). Originally, "mind" was not seen as a distinct entity from the body. Instead, it was defined as a specific function, "such as judging and directing actions" (p. 50). The mind that makes judgments or evaluations is called the evaluating mind, while the mind that directs actions according to the evaluations it has made is called the commanding mind.

Since the commanding mind takes its cues from the evaluating mind, the evaluating mind is the primary agent of one's proper behavior toward other people and thus of one's entrance "into a kind of communion with heaven" (Munro, 1982:58) or the Great Ultimate of which all men and things are a part. Proper action is dictated by *li*, the rules of conduct or principles, which are based on *yi*, moral sense, which in turn would lead to virtue or *de* by means of which one would come into harmony with Heaven or the Ultimate Source.

Cheng (1974) relates that de has "... the potency to incline man towards good acts in life" (p. 8). Mind is made of vital energy or vital nature (c. *qi*; j. *ki*) (Cheng, 1974) while "*li* conditions the possible permutations of [*qi*]" (Thompson, 1988: 32) and is neither distinct nor separable from *qi*. Although there has to be li for *qi* to exist, *li* does not have any control over *qi* once it has come into being (Kim, 1984).

Qi, according to Zhu Xi, constitutes and underlies everything in the world, both animate and inanimate. Qi is considered to be the source of life: "it moves or turns all the time and forms man and the 'ten thousand things.'" It is "both the material basis of all the things of the world and the ultimate source of the nonphysical or nonmaterial qualities, including life" (Kim, 1984: 28). Death results from the dispersion of this qi. Qi, then, has two major aspects: it can be formless, like heaven, or through "aggregation," it can acquire physical form and become man and everything else in the world (Kim, 1984).

Qi appears to be a multifaceted concept and there is no equivalent in English to indicate what the traditional Chinese thinkers meant by it. Kim (1984) observes that the terms or categories that the Westerner uses to describe qi are basically Western distinctions. They may have been alien to the Chinese way of thinking. To the Chinese, the various aspects of qi were inseparable and qi always meant all of these aspects at once when they used the word.

European Influence on Japanese Medicine

With the introduction of Christianity, Japan was also exposed to European sciences, especially medicine (Fujikawa, 1934). This is not to say, however, that Chinese medicine ceased to exercise its influence. Medicine in China, in the meantime, had undergone some changes (Wong et al., 1936). The etiology of diseases was classified into external and internal influences and into influences that did not belong to the previous two. Internal causes of diseases were disturbances of the seven emotions of joy, anger, grief, fear, love, hatred and desire. External factors included the influences of the wind, heat, moisture, fire and cold. The third category consisted of such things as hunger, overfeeding, drowning, insect bites, and so on.

European medicine was introduced into Japan by a Portuguese called Louis d'Almeida (1525–1583) and other missionaries as early as 1556 (Tuge, 1961). D'Almeida practiced and taught medicine and surgery at a temple in Funai (Bowers, 1970). The medicine that the Japanese were exposed to was based on the ancient Greek theory of the Four Cardinal Humors (Fujikawa, 1934). These humors consist of blood, choler, phlegm and black bile. In the right proportions, they would lead to good health, while an imbalance would cause illness. It was also believed, for instance, that the blood running from the liver was dark and thick, and that the digested food in the stomach would turn into blood in the small intestines.

European medicine received its chance to spread in Japan when the eighth Tokugawa shogun, Yoshimune (1684–1751; r. 1716–1745) changed the Japanese calendar and adopted the Western calendar (Bowers, 1970; Goodman, 1967). He also made sure that there was a sufficient supply of medicine available and he even initiated the building of a garden where medicinal plants could be cultivated. Eventually, he officially allowed the study of Dutch as well as Dutch medicine and science. During the period of isolation, the only European medicine practiced in Japan was basically Dutch medicine (Fujikawa, 1934). The Dutch were the only Westerners with whom the Japanese had any contact. Among the physicians at the Dutch factory on Deshima Island, however, were also some Germans. The Japanese were instructed by these Dutch and German physicians, but their influence was restricted to Nagasaki and Tokyo. In the beginning, Dutch medicine was transmitted to the Japanese by means of interpreters, which was not conducive to its development in Japan (Bowers, 1970). It was not until 1720 that Dutch books and manuscripts were allowed into Japan which, of course, greatly facilitated the expansion of Dutch science. The court librarians and physicians, in addition to the interpreters, were among the first to learn Dutch, which became the language of science in Japan at the time.

In exchange for what they learned from the Dutch, the interpreters gave them information about Japanese culture, geography, botany and medicine, the latter being mainly Chinese medicine. According to Lock (1980), although the Japanese would adopt Western medicine (especially surgery), they would still use the Chinese system for internal medicine, while Bowers (1970) related that modern anatomy did not begin to develop in Japan until two centuries after it had begun in Europe.

Under the influence of the Dutch, surgery (a sign of a reified view of the human body) became an accepted medical practice. In 1754, a physician by the name of Toyo Yamawaki (1705?–1762) observed the dissection of a beheaded criminal (Tuge, 1961). As a matter of fact, the Japanese did many dissections on corpses, mainly on those who were executed (Fujikawa, 1934). In 1771, two Japanese physicians, Maeno Ryotaku (1733–1803) and Sugita Gempaku (1738–1818), witnessed the autopsy of a decapitated criminal, which gave them the opportunity to compare descriptions provided in a Dutch book on anatomy (in Japan referred to as *Tafel Anotomia* [the original title being *Ontleedkundige Tafelen, Benevens de Daartoe Behoorende Afbeeldingen en Aanmerkingen Waarin het Samenstel des Menschenlijken Lichaams, en het Gebruik van Alle Deszelfs Deelen Afgebeeld Geleerd Word*]) with the organs themselves (Fujikawa, 1934; Tuge, 1961). The Dutch copy of the *Tafel Anatomia* was a translation of the German *Anatomische Tabellen* (*Anatomical Tables*) by Johann Adam Kulmus (1689–1745) of Breslau (Bowers, 1970). This book was published in 1722 in Danzig and the Dutch translation, called *Ontleed-kundige Tafelen*, was published in Amsterdam in 1734 by a surgeon from Leiden.

When Maeno and Sugita noticed that the book was more accurate than the older Chinese and Japanese works, they began a translation of the *Tafel* which took four years to complete. The Japanese translation—based on several other Western sources besides the *Tafel Anatomia*—was published in five volumes in 1774 and constituted a major breakthrough for Western medicine in Japan", because it showed that the anatomical theories from China were incorrect and that the rational basis of Western medicine and science was superior" (Bowers, 1970: 72). The title of the translation was *Kaitai Shinsho* (*New Book for Understanding the Human Body*) (Goodman, 1967). It was not until 1822, however, that surgery was taught on a more thorough basis. It is said that the first operation on someone under anesthesia was performed in 1805 by a Japanese, Hanaoka Seishu (1760–1836) (Tuge, 1961), using a lancet, scalpel, scissors, hammer, saw and chisel (Bowers, 1970).

After the publication of the Japanese translation of the *Tafel*, Western science increased in popularity and influence. European medicine, the Dutch language, natural history, astronomy and mathematics, for which Holland was now the center of knowledge instead of China, were referred to as "Dutch Study" (*Rangaku*) and were diligently pursued by a limited group of Japanese scholars (Bowers, 1970). Private medical schools were established in Tokyo, Kyoto and Osaka between 1786 and 1846. Some of the best students of these medical schools came from the samurai ranks (Lock, 1980).

In fact, becoming a physician, just like becoming a priest, was considered a suitable profession for the second and third sons of samurai. Studying medicine was also seen as a way for the lower classes to rise socially. Goodman (1967) observed that although the growth of Western learning was stimulated by the daimyo, the actual proponents of Western learning were the lower samurai who later became the leaders of modern Japan. Although the Japanese had mastered the basics of Western medicine, they still needed to know how to apply this knowledge. It was the German Philipp von Siebold (1796–1866), working for The Netherlands East Indies Army, who taught them to diagnose and treat diseases (Bowers, 1970). Von Siebold was the first Western physician to teach the Japanese systematically how to practice medicine. He is credited with performing the first Western-style cataract surgery in Japan (Bowers, 1970) and with the first breast amputation (Paul, 1984). His forte, however, was obstetrics and he is considered to be the "father of modern obstetrics in Japan" (Bowers, 1970; Paul, 1984).

As in the preceding period, the philosophical position of Tokugawa Japan was not in accordance with developments in the scientific fields, where an increasing objectification of the human body started to take place. It is true that by the Tokugawa Period man was seen as separate from nature an that the human body was opened, but it was also held that man was part of the Great Ultimate or the Original Source with which the individual has to become one in order to reach enlightenment. Unlike the practitioners of bujutsu, budo students had to strive to act in unison in order to get to know themselves. So, a shift in emphasis can be discerned, from the practitioner having to act as a whole to be able to survive on the battlefield to the individual having to become one with nature in order to self-actualize. The movements in the budo cannot be called functional anymore, but they are not intermediary movements either. It would probably be most accurate to call them expressive movements.

References

Anesaki, M. (1930). *History of Japanese religion*. London: Kegan Paul, Trench, Trubner and Co., Ltd.

Bellah, R. (1957). *Tokugawa religion: The values of pre-industrial Japan*. Glencoe, IL: The Free Press and The Falcon's Wing Press.

Bennett, L. (1976). *Reification of the human body in ancient Greece: A metabletic investigation*. Unpublished Ph.D. dissertation, University of Oregon, Eugene, OR.

Boodberg, P. (1953). The semasiology of some primary Confucian concepts. *Philosophy East and West, II*, 4: 317, 332.

Bowers, J. (1970). *Western medical pioneers in feudal Japan*. Baltimore: The John Hopkins Press.

Broekhoff, J. (1972). Physical education and the reification of the human body. *Gymnasion, IX*, 2: 4, 11.

Bunce, W. (1966). *Religions in Japan*. Rutland, VT: Charles E. Tuttle Co.

Chan, W. (1973). *A source book in Chinese philosophy*. Princeton, NJ: Princeton University Press.

Chang, C. (1974). Conscience, mind and individual in Chinese philosophy. *Journal of Chinese Philosophy, 2*, 1: 3–40.

Charpio, D. (1978). *The nature of human movement: A philosophical interpretation delineated from Neo-Confucianism*. Unpublished Ph.D. dissertation, University of North Carolina, Greensboro.

Daidoji, Y. (1984). *Budo shoshinshu*. (W. S. Wilson, Trans.). Burbank, CA: Ohara Publications, Inc.

Digel, H. (1986). Ueber den wandel der werte in gesellschaft, friezeit und sport. In K. Heinemann and H. Becker (Eds.), *Die zukunft des sports*. Schorndorf: Verlag Karl Hofmann, pp. 14–43.

Draeger, D. (1975). *Classical budo*. New York: Weatherhill.

Draeger, D. (1973). *Classical bujutsu*. New York: Weatherhill.

Fairbank, J., Reischauer, E. and Craig, A. (1973). *East Asia: Tradition and transformation*. London: George Allen & Unwin Ltd.

Fujikawa, Y. (1934). *Japanese medicine*. (John Riihrah, Trans.). New York: Paul B. Hoeber, Inc.

Fung, Y. (1983a). *A history of Chinese philosophy: Vol. I The period of the philosophers*. (Derk Bodde, Trans.). Princeton, NJ: Princeton University Press.

Fung, Y. (1983b). *A history of Chinese philosophy: Vol. II The period of classical learning*. (Derk Bodde, Trans.). Princeton, NJ: Princeton University Press.

Goodman, G. (1967). *The Dutch impact on Japan (1640–1853)*. Leiden: E. J. Brill.

Hammitzsch, H. (1980). *Zen in the art of the tea ceremony*. New York: Avon Books.

Herrigel, E. (1971). *Zen in the art of archery*. New York: Vintage Books.

Herrigel, G. (1983). *Zen in the art of flower arrangement*. London: Routledge and Kegan Paul, Ltd.

Hume, E. (1940). *The Chinese way in medicine*. Baltimore, MD: The John Hopkins Press.

Humphreys, C. (1960). *The way of action*. Baltimore, MD: Penguin Books Inc.

Kammer, R. (1978). *Zen and Confucius in the art of swordsmanship*. London: Routledge and Kegan Paul Ltd.

Kim, Y. (1984). Some aspects of the concept of ch'i in Chu Hsi. *Philosophy East and West, 34*, 1: 25–36.

Kitagawa, J. (1966). *Religion in Japanese history*. New York: Columbia University Press.

Kleinman, S. (Ed.). (1986). *Mind and body: East meets west*. Champaign, IL: Human Kinetics Publishers, Inc.

Koizumi, T. (1986). The importance of being stationary: Zen, relativity, and the aesthetics of no-action. In S. Kleinman (Ed.), *Mind and body: East meets west*. Champaign, IL: Human Kinetics Publishers, Inc.

Kurz, D. (1986). Von Sinn des sports. In K. Heinemann and H. Becker (Eds.) *Die Zukunft des sports*. Schorndorf: Verlag Karl Hofmann, pp. 44–68.

Lock, M. (1980). *East Asian medicine in urban Japan*. Berkeley, CA: University of California Press.

Mathews, R. (1975). *Mathew's Chinese-English dictionary*. Cambridge, MA: Harvard University Press.

Munro, D. (1982). *The concept of man in early China*. Stanford, CA: Stanford University Press.

Nelson, A. (1963). *The modern reader's Japanese-English character dictionary*. Rutland, VT: Charles E. Tuttle, Co.

Ono, S. (1981). *Shinto: The kami way*. Rutland, VT: Charles E. Tuttle, Co.

Paul, H. (1984). *Nederlanders in Japan, 1600–1857*. Weesp: Fibula-Van Dishoeck.

Pieter, W. (1987). Zen aesthetics and human movement. *Journal of Human Movement Studies, 13*, 8: 411–420.

Ratti, O. and Westbrook, A. (1979). *Secrets of the samurai: A survey of the martial arts in feudal Japan*. Rutland, VT: Charles E. Tuttle, Co.

Sansom, G. (1958). *A history of Japan to 1334*. Stanford, CA: Stanford University Press.

Sansom, G. (1961). *A history of Japan 1334–1615*. Stanford, CA: Stanford University Press.

Sansom, G. (1963). *A history of Japan 1615–1867*. Stanford, CA: Stanford University Press.

Schmidt, R. J. (1986). Japanese martial arts as spiritual education. In S. Kleinman (Ed.), *Mind and body: East meets west*. Champaign, IL: Human Kinetics Publishers, Inc., pp. 69–74.

Seward, J. (1984). *Hara-kiri: Japanese ritual suicide*. Rutland, VT: Charles E. Tuttle, Co.

Shih, H. (1953). Ch'an (Zen) Buddhism in China: Its history and method, *Philosophy East and West, III*, 1: 3–24.

Shih, H. (1931). The development of Zen Buddhism in China, *Chinese Social and Political Science Review, 15*, 4: 475–505.

Shute, C. (1968). The comparative phenomenology of Japanese painting and Zen Buddhism, *Philosophy East and West, XVIII*, 4: 285–298.

Spiessbach, M. (1991). Bodhidharma: Meditating monk, martial arts master or make-believe, *Journal of Asian Martial Arts, 1*, 4: 10–27.

Suzuki, D. (1974). The role of nature in Zen Buddhism. In H. B. Earhart (Ed.), *Religion in the Japanese experience: Sources and interpretations*. Belmont, CA: Wadsworth Publishing Co., pp. 131–134.

Suzuki, D. (1973). *Zen and Japanese culture*. Princeton, NJ: Princeton University Press.

Thompson, K. (1988). Li and yi as immanent: Chu Hsi's thought in practical perspective, *Philosophy East and West, 38*, 1: 30–46.

Tiwald, H. (1981). *Psycho-training im kampf-und budo-sport*. Ahrensburg bei Hamburg: Verlag Ingrid Czwalina.

Tu, W. (1971). The neo-Confucian concept of man, *Philosophy East and West, XXI*, 1:79–87.

Tuge, H. (Ed.). (1961). *Historical development of science and technology in Japan*. Tokyo: Kokusai Bunka Shinkokai.

Watts, A. (1957). *The way of Zen*. New York: Vintage Books.

Wong, K. and Wu, L. (1936). *History of Chinese medicine*. Shanghai: National Quarantine Service.

Yamamoto, T. (1979). *Hagakure*. (W. S. Wilson, Trans.). New York: Avon Books.

Swordsmanship and Esoteric Spirituality: An Introduction to Gerard Thibault's *Academie de l'Espee*

by John Michael Greer, B.A.

One of the illustration for Thibault's book, the Academy of the Sword, by a Flemish engraver. Illustrations supplied by Donald LaRocca, Associate Curator, Arms and Armor. *Courtesy of the Thomas J. Watson Library, Metropolitan Museum of Art.*

The relation between Asian martial arts and Western combat systems has been understood in sharply different ways over the last century or so. In 1887, Arthur Conan Doyle could simply describe a derivative of jujutsu as "Japanese wrestling," implying that whatever the differences in technique, Asian and European fighting methods could still be placed in the same general categories (Tracy, 1977: 25; Barton-Wright, 1899: 268–275, 402–410).[1] By contrast, toward the middle of the twentieth century, Asian combat systems came to be seen in the West as a set of exotic practices somehow connected to the "Eastern wisdom" of Asian spiritual traditions, and thus radically different from anything Western cultures had to offer. The term "martial art" itself came into common use on the wings of this perception; until quite recently it was rare to see the phrase used for any combat system originating outside East Asia.

More recently the pendulum has moved back the other way to some degree. Much of the hype and confusion surrounding Asian martial arts, not to mention Asian spiritual traditions, has been cleared away as these have become more familiar in the West. Equally, it has become increasingly clear that Western combat systems in the Middle Ages, Renaissance, and early modern periods had much in common with their Asian equivalents.

One distinction between East and West that has seemed solid up to the present, though, has to do with the presence of systems of combat rooted in philosophical and spiritual traditions of inner development. Hype or no hype, many Asian martial arts do fall into this category, some (for example, taijiquan and other Chinese arts of the *neijia* or Inner School) deriving much of their theory and practice from spiritual teachings (Schipper, 1993).[2] In the Western world, by contrast, connections of this sort have been thought to be absent.

This situation has recently been transformed by the discovery that at least one European combat system had deep connections to mystical and occult teachings. This recognition was the work of joy Hancox (1992: 46–48, 203–205), whose study of a tradition of mystical geometry led her to the inner basis of the most enigmatic text in the history of Western swordsmanship, Gerard Thibault's *Academie de l'Espee* (*Academy of the Sword*), originally published in 1630.[3] The present author's research has confirmed and expanded Hancox' original insight. In the course of translating Thibault's text and putting his methods into practice, it has become clear that his system—which has called forth baffled responses from many modern historians of fencing—makes sense only if it is understood as a martial art rooted in Western esoteric spirituality (Castle, 1969: 67–73).

The rediscovery of this dimension of Thibault's system has relevance to the scholarly study of martial arts generally (as well as to the study of Western esoteric traditions), but it also has a special relevance to students of Asian martial arts. Up to the present, East Asian traditions have provided the only known examples of deep interconnection between the martial arts and esoteric spirituality, and those examples are inevitably colored by the distinctive cultural patterns of mysticism and combat in China, Japan, and other Asian societies.

Coming as it does from the very different setting of Renaissance Europe, Thibault's swordsmanship system embodies radically different assumptions about spirituality, combat, and their potential connections. It therefore casts a new light on the entire range of issues implied by the spiritual dimensions of the martial arts.

Western and Eastern Esotericism

Several factors have played a role in obscuring the inner side of Thibault's swordsmanship. One of these is a tendency, pervasive in Western cultures since the Scientific Revolution, to dismiss the esoteric spirituality of the West as a body of superstitions unworthy of serious study. It is still common to find scholars with solid backgrounds in comparative religion, who are highly familiar with Buddhist, Daoist, and other non-Western traditions of inner transformation, but have never heard of equivalent Western systems such as Neo-Platonism or Cabala (Faivre, 1994). However, another obscuring factor is more central to the present study.

While there are important similarities between the esoteric traditions of Asia and Western Europe, the differences are also significant. One crucial distinction is found in the relative importance of ideas of intrinsic or subtle energy. Concepts of this sort are central to many Asian spiritual traditions, and thus play an equally central role in many Asian martial arts.[4] While the idea of subtle energy does occur in European thought, it has typically had a much less central place—particularly in the traditions of spiritual practice that form the bridge between esoteric philosophy and the martial arts.[5] For example, many Asian methods of meditation give a great deal of attention to issues of posture, breathing, and the flow of subtle energies through the body. In some traditions (for example, Daoist "breath circulation"), subtle energy work is the primary focus of meditative practice.

By contrast, few European methods of meditation paid more than cursory attention to such issues until quite recent times. Typically, the major focus of older Western meditative methods was on perceiving and understanding aspects of existence beyond the material. The standard methods included contemplation of symbolic images and training in philosophic modes of thought. The body and its subtle energies played little if any role in this work.[6]

This difference in focus must be grasped to make sense of the corresponding difference between Gerard Thibault's swordsmanship and Asian martial arts. The primary esoteric element in Thibault's system is not energetic but conceptual. Like many Asian martial arts, it bases itself on teachings concerning the hidden reality that underlies ordinary experience. However, in the West, that reality was not generally understood in terms of interactions of subtle energies. Rather, in the teachings from which Thibault's fencing derived, it was seen as a structure of transcendent ideas or patterns a structure traditionally expressed in terms of geometry.

Geometry has had a place in Western esoteric traditions since the time of Pythagoras, who taught a doctrine of mystical mathematics in the late seventh century BCE (Guthrie, 1988, Burkert, 1972). At various points in the history of Western esoteric spirituality, the Pythagorean tradition has played a significant role, but never so centrally as in the Renaissance. Pythagorean geometry was one of the few branches of ancient Greek and Roman mystical tradition that the Christian Church accepted and incorporated into its own synthesis, with results that can be seen in the magnificent Gothic cathedrals of medieval Europe (Flint, 1991; Lesser, 1957).

To this medieval heritage was added a substantial body of teaching rediscovered with the resurgence of classical learning at the beginning of the Renaissance. As a result, Pythagorean ideas came to be part of the common currency of thought all through Renaissance Europe (Hersey, 1976; Yates, 1969). At the same time, the importance of geometry to architects and engineers during the same period meant that geometrical ideas formed an obvious bridge between the esoteric and the practical—a bridge that architects, in particular, used constantly all through the Renaissance (Hersey, 1976).

Gerard Thibault and Academie de L'Espée

Gerard Thibault d'Anvers, painter, physician, and architect as well as master swordsman—the phrase "Renaissance man" comes irresistibly to mind—was born in 1574 in Antwerp. The names of his fencing teachers have not been preserved, as European martial traditions paid less attention to issues of lineage than their Asian equivalents, but he would have had the opportunity to study with masters of the Spanish school of fencing; Spain at that time ruled the Netherlands, and Spanish fencers had a continent-wide reputation as lethal duelists. Certainly the approach to fencing preserved in Thibault's book bears many similarities to the Spanish style, with the upright stance and the use of a circle to govern footwork being only the most obvious connections.[7]

The Spanish style was one of several new schools of fencing that had arisen out of a revolution in the arts of combat then under way in Europe. Central to that revolution was the abandonment of the heavy medieval broadsword and shield for a new style of weapon, the rapier, with a lighter, longer blade and a set of metal bars around the hilt to protect hand and wrist. The new rapier swordsmanship relied far more on thrusts than on cutting blows; and, in the Spanish school and some others, drew heavily on geometry as a theoretical basis. It is not hard to see why: the rapier is the most geometrical of weapons, a straight line moved through space to intersect another line or to penetrate the surface of the opponent's body. It was in this context, certainly, that Thibault himself came to understand the art of fencing.

In 1611, Thibault presented himself before the acknowledged Dutch fencing masters in a competition in Antwerp and took first prize. Summoned before Prince Maurice of Nassau to demonstrate his skill, he defeated all comers in a famous exhibition that lasted several days. The resulting reputation and financial support enabled him to begin work on a systematic manual of his approach to swordsmanship. *Academie de l'Espée*, produced with the support of the Holy Roman Emperor, the King of France, and a galaxy of lesser notables, was more than a decade in production and was finally published one year after Thibault's death in 1629 (de la Fontaine de Verwey, 1978).

Nearly four hundred folio pages long, illustrated with forty-nine doublepage engravings each showing a dozen or more images of fencing technique, the original edition of *Academie de l'Espée* may well be the largest and most ornate book on swordsmanship ever written. It was republished once, in a much less lavish form, in 1660. By that time, however, the Spanish school had begun to wane in popularity; the Italian school, ancestral to modem sport fencing, was well on its way to dominance. At the same time, Renaissance traditions of mystical geometry were of increasingly little interest to a society whose attention had been caught by the successes of the Scientific Revolution (Yates, 1964). While esoteric spiritual traditions played an important role all through Renaissance culture, they were thrust to the intellectual and cultural fringes of the Western world as the modem period dawned. Correspodingly, Thibault's work was entirely forgotten except by a few historians of the literature of swordsmanship until quite recent times.

Elements of Thibault's Method

Trying to reconstruct an extinct martial art from a written description is a difficult task. In the present case, that task is made easier by the extraordinary level of detail in Thibault's book. The techniques in *Academie de l'Espée* are presented with a thoroughness unmatched by other contemporary fencing manuals; positions and movements are marked against an intricate geometric pattern, and such details as shifts of body weight from leg to leg and the relative pressure of one sword against the other are covered wherever relevant. It is thus possible not only to describe but also to practice most of Thibault's techniques with some assurance.

Summary of the Basic Principles of Thibault's Approach to Swordsmanship

I. Geometrical proportion.
"[A]ll the measures and stances to be observed in this practice," Thibault proclaims near the beginning of his book, "proceed from the proportions of the human body" (Thibault, 1998: 10, 17). These proportions give rise to the "mysterious circle," the complex geometrical pattern used to teach swordsmanship; to the proper length of the sword; to the three Instances, or combat distances; and even to such

apparently minor details as the design of the hanger and cincture that support the rapier from the sword belt. In Thibault's system, each fencer uses his own height as the basic unit of measure, with every other factor unfolding from this by way of a series of geometrical operations.

2. Natural posture and movement.

Thibault criticized the fencing styles of his day for a reliance on unnatural stances. "I have seen that people are accustomed by all of these styles to strange postures: the body bent in several angles with feet and legs put out of their natural proportion, and in postures wholly repugnant to the ordinary way one walks or stands. Instead of showing any great courage by these postures, in fact, those who use them inconvenience themselves and lessen their own force" (Thibault. 1998: 10, 17). Thibault's own posture, based on that of the Spanish school, is an upright stance with the feet one foot-length apart, the toes slightly angled outward, and the sword and arm extended straight out toward the opponent. All his footwork, similarly, is based on the ordinary walking pace.

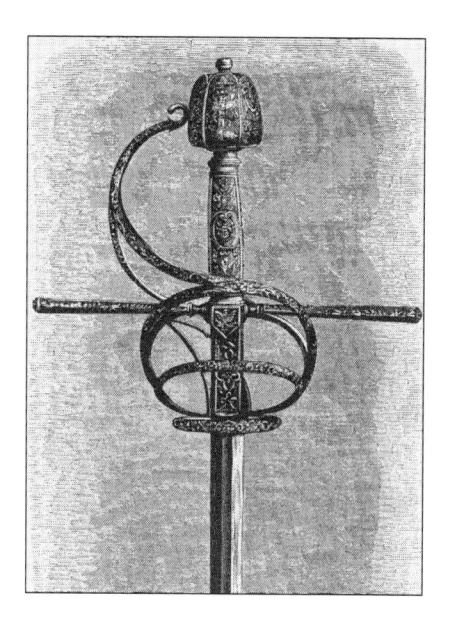

3. Use of sentiment.

In fencing, the French word *sentiment* ("awareness" or "sensitivity"), implies a fine degree of sensitivity to the pressure of one blade against the other. To Thibault, sentiment is the key to all close combat. Accordingly, and in flat contradiction to contemporary practice, he instructs the student to keep his blade in contact with the opponent's, using the second "weight" —that is, the lightest possible degree of pressure—to maintain contact. "Once we have contact between the blades, we are able to make our approaches against the adversary with assurance, since we are certain always to know in time the designs which he makes against us: no sooner are these begun than we have already prepared ourselves against them" (Thibault, 1630: ch. 9 p. 12). Mastery of sentiment makes it possible to "subject" the opponent's blade, controlling its movements. In turn, the key to sentiment is a matter of footwork and the proper position of the body.

4. Unity of attack and defense.
Like most early fencing manuals, Thibault's book teaches few purely defensive techniques. Instead, nearly all of his techniques combine attack and defense: thrusts are made at angles that simultaneously ward off the adversary's attacks, and footwork is designed to move the body out of danger and create openings for an immediate response at the same time. In some of Thibault's most typical techniques, an attack is deflected and the attacker cut down in a single motion. Similarly, in the last or "execution" stage of most techniques the opponent's sword is forced out of line by the same movement that delivers the final killing thrust, making it impossible for him to counterattack even in his death throes.

5. Constant motion.
Static postures play a role in training, but Thibault cautions that they are not to be used in actual combat: "Let [the student] continue always to move, using a free and natural pace, toward one or the other of the two sides... [a]s soon as he comes into measure, let him assure himself of his opponent's sword, by attacking it to subject it, or by binding it, or by covering it, or by carrying out an estocade of first intention along it, if this is convenient, continuing to move always without interruption" (Thibault, 1998: 49). Constant movement was also one of the most noted features of the Spanish school from which Thibault's system was derived.

6. Control of the centerline.
One of the major strategic issues in Thibault's fencing was the centerline—the "Straight Line," in his terminology—measuring the shortest distance between the two opponents. To hold the centerline is to close it against the opponent's attacks, forcing him to use slower, more roundabout trajectories that can more easily be countered or forestalled. Should the opponent leave the centerline unguarded, at least two immediate options present themselves: first, "entering within the angle," a movement similar to the *irimi* technique of aikido, which slips past his point and permits a variety of attacks, including grappling moves that seize or pin the hilt of his sword; and second, an "*estocade* [straight thrust] of first intention," which strikes along the open centerline to a vital target.

7. Alternation of line and circle.

Like the geometry on which it is based, Thibault's fencing system relies on a combination of straight lines and circular movements. Most of the attacks are made along straight lines of least distance, and the basic posture extends the sword straight out toward the opponent along the centerline; still, circular attacks and a variety of cuts also play a significant role. In the same way, footwork includes both linear and circular movements; for example, it is very common for a fencer using Thibault's system to step straight with one leg and bring the other one after it along an arc, shifting to a more advantageous angle.

8. Predominance of the mind.

In many ways, the most important feature of Thibault's method, and the one that links it most closely to Western esoteric traditions, is its reliance on the mental dimension. Thibault dismissed the purely physical approach to fencing as inadequate: "It is hardly surprising that those who do not aspire to any science of arms, but try to succeed solely by long and continual exercises in quickness of the body and of the arm, by which they are able to prevail by forestalling and taking advantage of opponents rather than by compelling them, do not comprehend the secrets of so noble a weapon" (Thibault, 1998: 49). From his standpoint, strength and speed are of small importance, and the fencer who relies on either one is likely to come to grief. In fact, Thibault cautions the student against "wasting his movements by an ill-advised quickness" (Thibault, 1630: ch. lip. 5), and provides plenty of counters to use against those who try to force their way out of a situation by simple strength. In the Pythagorean teachings of Renaissance esoteric spirituality, the realm of matter is passive, shaped and governed by the realm of Nous, the transcendent Mind. In the same way, in Thibault's system of swordsmanship, the opponent is first conquered mentally, and his physical defeat follows inevitably after.

Notes

1. The art of baritsu, "the Japanese system of wrestling," is mentioned in one of Doyle's Sherlock Holmes stories as a skill possessed by the great detective. Doyle derived this from "bartitsu," a version of jujutsu developed by (and named after) the Englishman E. W. Barton-Wright, and introduced to England in 1899.
2. The English-language literature on the interface between Asian martial arts and esoteric spirituality is immense, though dwarfed by that in several other languages. For the relation between Daoism and Chinese martial arts, see especially Kristofer Schipper (1993).
3. The first eight chapters have been published in an English translation by the present author (1998), and the remainder will be published in three additional volumes by the same press. All quotes from the first eight chapters are from the published translation, cited as Thibault, 1998; all quotes from the remainder of the text are original translations made for this article, and cited as Thibault, 1630.
4. The Chinese term *qi*, its Japanese cognate *ki*, and its partial Sanskrit equivalent *prana* are typical.
5. The Latin word *spiritus*, "spirit" or" breath," was the standard term for intrinsic energy in European medieval and Renaissance sources. More recent traditions in the West have made use of coined words such as *od* or *vril*, relied on transliterated Asian terms, or borrowed words such as "ether" and "magnetism" from the terminology of contemporary science.
6. Classic accounts of Western meditative practice may be found in the writings of Neoplatonist philosophers such as Plotinus (204–270 CE) and Iamblichus (c. 250-c. 325 CE) and in early Cabalistic works such as the anonymous Sepher Yetzirah. For modern accounts of Western esoteric meditative traditions, see Greer (1996), Bardon (1962), Kaplan (1982), and Knight (1995).
7. The question of an esoteric dimension to the Spanish school as a whole must be left open at this time. Spain was as influenced by the Pythagorean revival of the Renaissance as any other European country, but the constant presence of the Inquisition made Spanish practitioners of esoteric spirituality more than usually interested in keeping out of sight. A translation of *De la Filosofia de las Armas* (1582), the major work by the Spanish fencing master Jeronimo de Carranza, is reportedly in preparation and may shed light on this issue.

Reference

Bardon, F. (1962). *Initiation into hermetics.* Kettig uber Koblenz, Germany: Osiris.

Barton-Wright, E. (1899). The new art of self-defence. *Pearson's Magazine 7*, pp. 268–275, 402–410.

Burkert, W. (1972). *Lore and science in early Pythagoreanism.* Cambridge, MA: Harvard University Press.

Castle, E. (1969). *Schools and masters of fence.* York, PA: Shumway.

de la Fontaine de Verwey, H. (1978, Autumn). Gerard Thibault and his academie de l'espée. *Quaerendo VIII.*

Faivre, A. (1994). *Access to Western esotericism.* Albany, NY: State University of New York Press.

Flint, V. (1991). *The rise of magic in early medieval Europe.* Princeton: Princeton University Press.

Greer, J. (1996). *Paths of wisdom.* St. Paul: Llewellyn.

Greer, J. (1998). *Academy of the sword: A Renaissance handbook of hermetic swordsmanship, Part one: Philosophy and practice.* Seattle, WA: Fir Mountain Press.

Guthrie, W. (Ed.), (1988). *The Pythagorean sourcebook and library.* Grand Rapids: Phanes.

Hancox, J. (1992). *The Byrom collection.* London: Jonathan Cape.

Hersey, G. (1976). *Pythagorean palaces: Magic and architecture in the Italian Renaissance.* Ithaca, NY: Cornell University Press.

Kaplan, A. (1982). *Meditation and kabbalah.* York Beach, ME: Weiser.

Knight, G. (1995). *Experience of the inner worlds.* York Beach, ME: Weiser.

LaRocca, D. (1998). *The academy of the sword: Illustrating fencing books 1500–1800.* New York: The Metropolitan Museum of Art.

Lesser, G. (1957). *Gothic cathedrals and sacred geometry.* London: Alec Tiranti.

Schipper, K. (1993). *The Taoist body.* Berkeley: University of California Press.

Thibault D'Anvers, G. (1630). *Academie de l'espee.* Leiden: Elzevier.

Tracy, J. (1977). *Encyclopedia Sherlockiana.* New York: Doubleday.

Yates, F. (1964). *Giordano Bruno and the hermetic tradition.* Chicago: University of Chicago Press.

Yates, F. (1969). *Theatre of the world.* Chicago: Chicago University Press.

Kindred Spirits:
The Art of the Sword in Germany and Japan

by S. Matthew Galas, Esq.

In the foreground, a swordsman defends against his opponent's *oberhau* (downwards cut) by striking his arm. To the left, another swordsman parries a similar attack with a *zwerchhau* (horizontal cut). This cut simultaneously deflects the incoming blade and strikes the opponent's head. *All illustrations courtesy of S. M. Galas.*

Background

Historians and anthropologists have long recognized the many similarities between the cultures of feudal Japan and medieval Europe. The government by a feudal hierarchy based on military service, the domination of the battlefield by an elite warrior class with a strict code of conduct, the cultivation of arts and letters alongside the use of weapons—all of these subjects have been noted and discussed at length. Less attention, however, has been paid to the close parallels between the fighting arts of the European knight and the samurai of feudal Japan. This chapter will examine the art of the sword in medieval Germany, comparing and contrasting it with the classical Japanese martial traditions (*ryuha*). The period covered by this inquiry will reach from approximately 1350 until 1600. For the sake of brevity, the focus will be on general principles and combat philosophy rather than on specific techniques.

The student of the Japanese tradition is fortunate, since the martial arts of the classical warrior (*bushi*) have been handed down to the present as a living art. As a result, he need only look to surviving sword fighting schools (*kenjutsu*) for illumination. Despite this advantage, changes in the form of the Japanese sword, as well as the incremental modification of techniques by successive headmasters, make it difficult to determine whether the kenjutsu of today is truly the same as that practiced by the warriors of medieval Japan.

The European tradition presents even greater difficulty. The martial systems of medieval Europe are long dead, victims of the invention of gunpowder and firearms. Modern fencing offers no clues, derived as it is from the featherweight gentleman's sword of the 18th century. Further hindering this study is a host of stereotypes and misconceptions concerning the knight's armor and weapons.

Fortunately, these European arts are not lost, but merely forgotten. Although their existence has gone largely unnoticed, a whole series of medieval treatises on the art of the sword has survived to the present day. Approximately sixty in number, these *fechtbuecher* (fencing manuals) contain the accumulated teachings of generations of German sword masters. The first of these manuals was written in 1389; the last of the series in 1612. The works of these German masters allow a detailed glimpse into the principles and techniques of what they called the *kunst des fechtens*—the art of fighting.

A Brief History

Nearly all of the surviving German manuals bear the mark of Johannes Liechtenauer, an influential sword master of the 14th century.[1] Liechtenauer travelled throughout Europe, studying under the finest swordsmen he could find. Returning to Germany, he systematized and perfected the lessons he had learned. Obsessed with secrecy, Liechtenauer consolidated his teachings into a series of verses so cryptic that only those initiated into their meaning could decipher them. Gathering a select group of students around him, the master taught his secrets to a chosen few.

After Liechtenauer's death, his disciples grew concerned about the growing corruption of the art by lesser masters. Dropping the veil of secrecy, they began writing manuals which interpreted the great master's verses and explained his rules of swordsmanship. For the next 250 years, German masters used these verses as a framework for teaching the art of the long sword.

During the 15th century, some of these masters enjoyed the patronage of the highest ranks of German nobility. Sigmund Ringeck taught swordsmanship to the powerful dukes of Bavaria, Ott the Jew served as wrestling master for the Hapsburg archdukes of Austria, while Hans Talhoffer tutored the nobility of Swabia. The prestige of these masters ensured the spread of Liechtenauer's teachings throughout Germany, Austria, and eastern Europe.

Aside from Johannes Liechtenauer, two other masters profoundly influenced the fighting arts of medieval Germany. The first of these was Ott the Jew, a wrestling master whose techniques were used to supplement the weapon arts. The second was Hans Lecküchner, a priest who adapted Liechtenauer's long sword techniques to suit the *messer*, a one-handed, machete-like weapon. The writings of both these masters were considered authoritative and were widely copied.[2]

Assisting the spread of Liechtenauer's teachings in the 15th century was the foundation of an influential, guild-like association of swordsmen known as the *Marxbrueder* (Brotherhood of Saint Mark). From their seat in the city of Frankfurt am Main, the Marxbrueder organized the teaching of the art and the licensing of new masters. Since many members of this organization were merchants, the practice of the *ritterliche kunst* (the knightly art) rapidly spread to the middle class.[3]

The advent of the printing press further assisted the dissemination of the art. The first printed book on the *Kunst des Fechtens* was published in Vienna, Austria, in 1516. This work proved so popular that it was even translated into French.[4] Thereafter, printed fencing manuals proliferated.

During the 16th century, the most prominent masters gravitated towards the great cities of Germany. Augsburg, Frankfurt, Nuremberg, and Strasbourg all were home to influential masters who published treatises on swordsmanship and the other martial arts. In 1570, the greatest of the later masters, Joachim Meyer, published an important manual in Strasbourg. This printed work was reprinted in 1600 and was widely distributed throughout Germany.

By the end of the 16th century, firearms had become so efficient that body armor was nearly useless. As the use of armor steadily declined, so too, did the need for a sword heavy enough to cope with it. In turn, the comparatively lightweight rapier became increasingly popular, eventually eclipsing the older, knightly weapon. The last manual of this series, published in 1612, devotes twice as much space to the rapier as it does to the long sword. Thereafter, fencing manuals tended to ignore the long sword, until it faded from the scene around the end of the 17th century.

In Japan, the oldest surviving school of swordsmanship is the Tenshin Shoden Katori Shinto-ryu.[5] Its founder, Iizasa Choisai Ienao (1387–1488), was born around the same time that Liechtenauer died in Germany. Choisai was one of a number of prominent Japanese swordsman who appeared in the 14th and 15th centuries. Like Johannes Liechtenauer, Choisai and his contemporaries were the product of chaotic social conditions and unceasing war, which brought about a flowering of the martial arts in both cultures.

However, this blossoming of swordsmanship took different paths in the two cultures. In Germany, Johannes Liechtenauer cast a shadow of influence that lasted well over two centuries. So great was his reputation that his teachings were almost universally adopted. Although a few masters varied from the mainstream in their interpretation of the great master's verses, there was essentially one unified system of swordsmanship throughout the German-speaking lands.

In contrast, Japan developed hundreds of competing schools, each with its own combat theory, philosophy, and techniques. Although the martial arts community outside of Japan tends to focus on Iizasa Choisai Ienao, he was merely one example of a much larger trend in Japanese society. The Katori Shrine, which his school is named after, was a flourishing center of martial training for decades before Choisai began his studies there. Other centers, such as the nearby Kashima Shrine, were just as important to the development of swordsmanship in Japan. Furthermore, other sword masters such as Tsukahara Bokuden, Hidetsuna Kamiizumi, and the Yagyu family played equally important roles in the development of kenjutsu. As a result, there is no single figure comparable to Johannes Liechtenauer who can be labeled as the father of Japanese swordsmanship.

In time, the introduction of firearms profoundly affected the martial arts of both countries. In the forward to his manual of 1570, Joachim Meyer attributes the decline in the art of the long sword to the widespread use of firearms, ". . . with which the most manly and valiant hero is sometimes robbed of his life . . . by the least and most cowardly."[6] The continuous wars of central Europe ensured that this trend continued, leading to the demise of the art.

In Japan, the introduction of firearms contributed instead to the survival of the sword-art. In 1575, a scant five years after Meyer voiced his complaint, General Oda Nobunaga's masses of harquebusiers won a crushing victory over classical bushi at the battle of Nagashino. The decisive effect of the new weapon paved the way for the unification of Japan under the Tokugawa shogunate. Ironically, the peace brought about by the advent of the gun allowed the Japanese art of the long sword to survive and flourish—the opposite effect that it had in Europe.

The arrival of Dutch and Portuguese traders in the mid-16th century marked a period of contact and cultural exchange between the Japanese and the various countries of Europe. In particular, European military technology was a matter of keen interest to the Japanese. To what extent 16th century Japanese swordsmen studied European styles of fencing, however, is a matter of conjecture. Some have speculated that the various *ni to* (two sword) styles which later flourished in Japan were inspired by the rapier and dagger fencing which was so popular among Spanish, Portuguese, and Dutch swordsmen of the time.

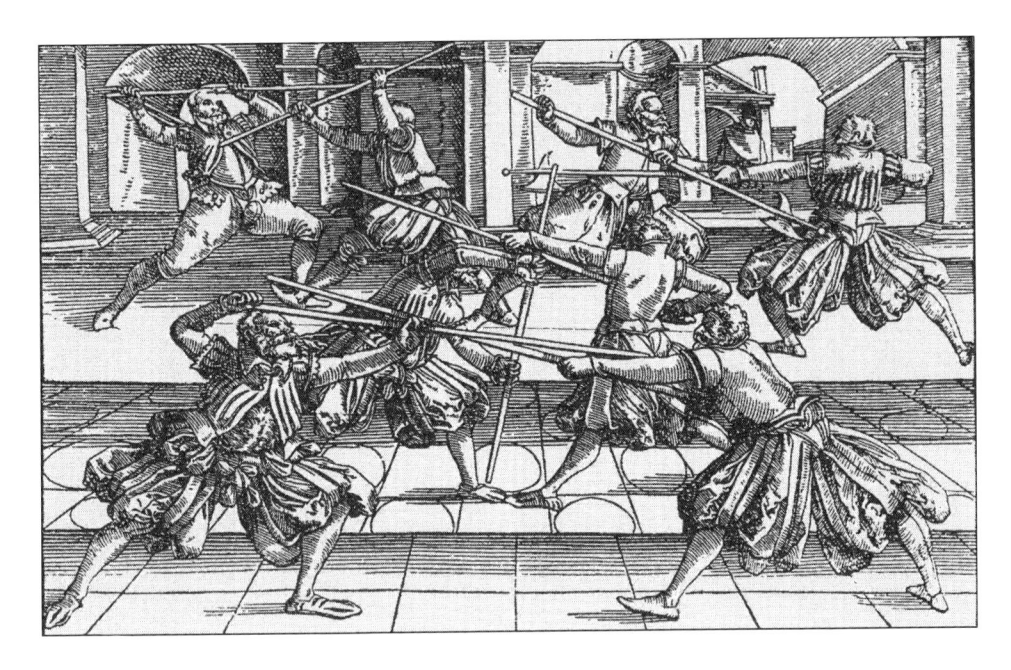

Techniques using quarterstaff and halbard, from Joachim Meyer's manual of 1570.

Any connection between European and Japanese long sword techniques is more tenuous still. The use of the long sword was rapidly declining in Europe during the late 16th and early 17th centuries. Instead, European fencing masters of the time devoted themselves to refining the use of the rapier; the long sword was increasingly dismissed as an anachronism. Although the long sword remained popular much longer in Germany than elsewhere in Europe, the number of German visitors to Japan during this period was insignificant.[7] Thus, the likelihood of any significant borrowing or exchange of long sword techniques appears minimal at best.

An Overview of the German Sword Art

The German masters divided their techniques into three major categories: *blossfechten* (unarmored combat), *harnisch fechten* (combat in armor), and *rossfechten* (mounted combat). The most important weapon in each category was the long sword, since the principles of its use were considered applicable to all other weapons. Against unarmored foes, the long sword was used with both hands to cut, thrust, and parry. Against armored opponents, the swordsman grasped the middle of the blade with his left hand, while his right hand gripped the hilt. Held in this manner, the sword was used like a short spear, enabling forceful, accurate thrusts to be aimed at gaps in the opponent's armor. A third method was used when mounted; the swordsman wielded his sword in one hand, while managing the horse's reins with the other.

Liechtenauer's verses concentrate on the principal knightly weapons: the spear, the long sword, and the dagger. Later masters expanded this repertoire to include a variety of other weapons as well. Foremost among these were the machete-like *messer*, the poleaxe or halbard, the staff, and the sword and buckler. The manuals cover each of these weapons in detail, including methods for disarming the opponent.

Alongside this arsenal of weapons, the German school placed a heavy emphasis on wrestling techniques. In addition to the usual techniques for dealing with an unarmed assailant, the manuals include detailed methods for neutralizing a knife-wielding opponent. Wrestling was fully integrated into weapons practice as well, with grappling and throwing techniques used at close quarters. Many works even describe techniques for wrestling on horseback, the object being to throw or drag the opponent from his mount.

The principal weapons of the classical bushi—tachi, tanto, yari, and naginata—are comparable in both form and function to the German long sword, dagger, spear, and poleaxe. Both cultures developed fencing systems for each of these weapons, including techniques for armored, unarmored, and (when applicable) mounted combat. Furthermore, both martial systems shared an emphasis on grappling techniques, whether armored or not. In a sense, both knights and samurai were generalists rather than specialists, since they were expected not only to be proficient in all weapons, but competent wrestlers as well.

One area where the two cultures differed was in their attitude towards archery. Although European knights were commonly taught to use both longbow and crossbow, they firmly believed that missile weapons were the domain of commoners. This disdain was best expressed by the author of one of the knightly epics: "A coward was he who first used the bow, for he feared to close with his enemy."[8] To the samurai, however, archery was a noble art, older and even more respected than the art of the sword.

Another difference is the inclusion of sword and buckler techniques in the German system. A buckler is a small, circular shield, perhaps a foot in diameter. The Japanese schools never seem to have emphasized this defensive weapon. Like their European counterparts, the Japanese bushi used large, standing shields to protect themselves against missile weapons, but for some reason they never adopted the shield in hand-to-hand combat.

The Development of the Long Sword

For centuries, the arms and armor of the European knight remained essentially unchanged. His armor consisted of chain mail and a shield; his weapons were a one-handed sword and a lance. A mounted warrior, the knight considered combat on foot the work of commoners. However, this status quo began to change in the late 13th century. The increasing use of crossbows and longbows—which could easily pierce chain mail—led to the development of heavier, more protective armor.[9] Furthermore, the appearance of disciplined bodies of infantry which could withstand a heavy cavalry charge forced the knight to fight some of his battles on foot.

These battlefield changes led to the development of a versatile new weapon, the long sword. Wielded with one hand on horseback, the long sword was used with two hands when fighting on foot. Generally measuring from four to four and a half feet in length, the new weapon was sturdy enough to cope with a fully armored opponent. However, its comparatively light weight of between three and four pounds made it useful against even unarmored foes.[10] Its straight, acutely-pointed, double-edged blade was equally well-adapted for cutting and thrusting. Wielded with one hand on horseback, the long sword had a long grip which allowed it to be used with two hands when fighting on foot.

First appearing in the 13th century, the long sword's versatility made it extremely popular with the knightly classes, both on the battlefield and off. In Germany, it became the principal knightly weapon until the abandonment of armor in the 17th century.[11]

Although the long sword is commonly thought of as a military weapon, contemporary artworks make clear that this weapon was also worn with civilian dress. Numerous paintings and woodcut prints depict men in civilian attire with long swords hanging at their sides or cradled under their arms. Thus, the long sword was not only an instrument of war, but was also used as a means of self-defense, both at home and on the street.

Fencing with the düsack, a single-edged blade with an integral guard. In the foreground, two stances. In the rear, grappling and trapping techniques. From Joachim Meyer's manual of 1570.

Like the long sword, the Japanese katana was an all-purpose weapon, designed for both one- and two-handed use, in both a military and civilian context. This unity of purpose resulted in startling parallels in technique between the German and Japanese schools of swordsmanship. For example, many of the stances used by these schools are identical. So are many of the basic cuts, thrusts, and parries. Furthermore, the styles of both nations have separate series of techniques specifically devised for armored and unarmored combat.

The most conspicuous difference between the two weapons is the curvature of the blade. The long sword has a straight blade, well-suited for thrusting. The katana's blade is curved, making for a more efficient cut.

A more significant difference between the two weapons is the number of edges. The long sword has a double-edged blade, while the katana is a single-edged weapon. As a result, German masters developed a variety of close-range attacks in which the back edge is used to make hooking cuts around an opponent's parry. The Japanese school lacks this series of techniques.

Another important difference is the length of the blade. The long sword's blade is approximately ten inches longer than that of the katana. This difference in length has a profound effect on technique once the swords are crossed. Since the katana has a shorter blade, it describes a shorter arc when cutting around to another target—resulting in greater speed. Conversely, the long German blade travels a longer arc when cutting to a new target—exposing the swordsman to the danger of a counterattack while he is in the midst of his cut. Thus, German sword techniques place a greater emphasis on maintaining blade contact once the swords have crossed, thrusting over or around the opponent's parry instead of cutting around to a new target. On the contrary, Japanese techniques seem to place more emphasis on leaving the opposing blade and striking around to a new target.

Finally, the two weapons are equipped with radically different styles of hilts. The long sword is equipped with a cross hilt, while the katana has a small, circular guard (tsuba). Compared to the minimalist tsuba, the long sword's cross hilt somewhat obstructs the free play of the wrists while cutting. However, the cross hilt allows a wide variety of parries and blade-trapping techniques that are impossible, or at least dangerous, with a tsuba.

Swordsmanship: Principles and Techniques

The remainder of this article will compare unarmored combat using the long sword with similar combat using the katana. For the sake of brevity, the focus will be on general principles and tendencies rather than on individual techniques. This comparison is made somewhat difficult by the sheer number of surviving Japanese ryuha, many of which have radically different combat philosophies. Another difficulty is the teaching method employed. The German masters used standard Western methodology, presenting general principles, and then applying them to individual techniques. The Japanese method takes the opposite approach, proceeding from the specific to the general. Thus, the underlying principles of Japanese swordsmanship are seldom made explicit. Instead, they must be deduced from the kata of the various ryuha.

Footwork

The German system considered proper coordination of hands and feet to be the foundation of good swordsmanship. When making a cut, a swordsman should always step forward with the foot on the same side that he is cutting from. Thus, if a swordsman intends to cut from the right side, he should initially position himself with his left foot forward. As he makes his cut, he should step forward with his right foot. The same applies when a swordsman desires to cut from the left; as he delivers the cut, he should step forward with his left foot. This cutting method allows the swordsman to put his body weight into the cut, while maintaining a balanced position. On the contrary, a swordsman who cuts from one side while stepping from the other places himself in a twisted, unbalanced position. This faulty cutting method also limits the range of his cut.

Other aspects of footwork include methods for sidestepping an opponent's attack, pivoting steps that enable a swordsman's attack to reach around an adversary's parry, and stepping patterns used to deceive an enemy.

The footwork used in the Japanese ryuha generally seems to conform to the same rule expressed by the German masters. Cuts from the right are usually made while stepping forward with the right foot, and vice versa. Most kenjutsu schools also make use of defensive footwork, such as sidesteps, to avoid an opponent's attack and diminish the force of his blow.

The Basic Cuts

According to Liechtenauer, only two basic types of cut can be made with the edge of the long sword. Cuts from above, travelling in a downward direction, are known as *oberhau* (over cuts). Cuts made from below, travelling upward, are known as *unterhau* (under cuts). Since these cuts can be delivered from either the right or left side, four basic cuts result. All other cuts are variations of these four basic cuts.[12]

Elaborating on the four cuts, the German masters taught their students to make cuts from eight directions. The downward cuts from either side can be made either vertically (*scheitelhau*) or diagonally (*zornhau*). Upward cuts can likewise be made either diagonally or vertically. Finally, cuts can also be made horizontally from either side (*zwerchhau* or *mittelhau*). Furthermore, each of these cuts can be made with either the front edge or the back edge of the blade. An eight-armed diagram, similar to an asterisk, was developed to illustrate the blade paths of these derivative cuts. Despite this complexity, the German masters emphasized that all of these techniques are simply variations of the four basic cuts mentioned above.

Instruction in the use of the rapier. Note the diagram on the wall, which shows the eight directions from which cuts can be made. Nearby statues are marked with vertical, diagonal, and horizontal lines to show the targets for various cuts.

The cuts used in the Japanese ryuha are quite similar to those of the German school. The diagonal downward cuts (*kesa-giri* and *gyaku-kesa*) correspond closely to the *zornhau* from right and left. Diagonal upward cuts from both sides, usually referred to as *kiri-age*, are common to kenjutsu as well. These are identical in form to the German *unterhau*. Furthermore, some of the more modern Japanese schools teach cuts from eight directions, even using an eight-armed diagram similar to the German one mentioned above.

On the other hand, Japanese schools tend to place much greater emphasis on vertical downward cuts (*kiri-otoshi*) than the German system. This is especially the case in Itto-ryu and its derivative schools, from which modern kendo evolved.

The Basic Thrusts

Despite the common misconception that thrusting techniques first appeared in the Renaissance, medieval sword masters fully appreciated the value of the thrust. Because of its speed and efficiency, the thrust was the preferred method for regaining the initiative after parrying an opponent's attack. In addition to the more typical thrusts along a straight line, the German manuals include techniques in which a cut is transformed into a thrust. The manuals refer to this variously as "throwing the point" or "making a thrust out of a cut."[13] This is accomplished by striking at the opponent's face or chest with the point of the sword, instead of the edge—much like a coupè in modern fencing.

As with the cuts, the German manuals divide thrusting techniques into two categories: thrusts from above (*obere ansetzen*) and thrusts from below (*untere ansetzen*). Since each type of thrust can be made from either the right or the left, four basic thrusts result. Thrusts from above are usually made with the hands held high, with the blade sloping downward towards the opponent. Thrusts from below are generally made with the hands held low, the blade inclining upward towards the adversary. When thrusting from the right, the swordsman's wrists are crossed; when thrusting from the left, his wrists are uncrossed.

Finally, the German repertoire contains one-handed thrusts with the sword. Releasing the grip with his right hand, the swordsman steps forward with his left foot. As he does so, his left hand launches the point forward at the opponent's face or chest.

Nearly all of these techniques appear, with greater or lesser frequency, in the kata of the various Japanese ryuha. The only exception seems to be the cuts with the point, which are rendered difficult by the curve of the Japanese blade. As mentioned earlier, the main difference between the thrusting techniques of the two national systems is the emphasis placed upon them. This emphasis, in turn, seems based on the varying characteristics of Japanese and German blades.

The Four Lines of Attack

Liechtenauer divided the human body into four lines of attack, a division still used in modern fencing. He did this by drawing two imaginary lines through the body: one vertical, through the center line, the other horizontal, under the ribs. These lines divide the body into four quarters, each with particular techniques devised to attack it. At their most basic, these openings can be broken down into the right and left side of the head, and the right and left side of the body under the arms. In foot and mounted combat, however, variations exist in the number of openings.

The swordsman typically attacks the lower openings with an *unterhau* (under cut). When attacking the upper openings, the swordsman uses either an *oberhau* (over cut) or a *zwerchhau* (cross cut), a horizontal blow. Of these two, the *zwerchhau* is preferred, since the uplifted hilt provides better cover for the swordsman's head. Given a choice, a good swordsman always attacks the upper openings. Not only are these targets closer to him, but they are also harder to defend. In addition, a successful hit on the upper openings is far more likely to be lethal than a blow to the lower areas.

The Japanese schools lack a similar division of the body, concentrating instead on striking at the opponent's center. The targets of the basic cuts differ as well. For example, diagonal downward cuts such as *kesa-giri* are usually aimed at the juncture of the neck and shoulder, rather than the side of the head. Upward cuts (*kiriage*), however, are usually aimed at the sides of the body underneath the arms, much like the German *unterhau*. Although no explicit teachings seem to exist in kenjutsu regarding the relative merit of cuts to the upper and lower body, the kata in most schools clearly favor cuts delivered at the upper body.[14]

The Stances

The German masters sternly warned against tarrying in the stances, since they believed a swordsman is better off attacking his opponent than lingering in a static position. One master observed that the stances are really nothing more than certain points in the course of an attack, at which the swordsman momentarily pauses to see whether he should continue with his current course of action or change course. This German disdain for tarrying in a stance is mirrored in the Japanese schools. In Yagyu Shinkage-ryu, for example, instructors emphasize that there are *no kamae* (stances), only *kurai*, which are explained as fleeting, momentary positions connected by techniques.

According to German theory, each stance has particular techniques best suited to it, as well as unique weaknesses. If he is familiar with the stances, a swordsman can predict his opponent's actions with a fair degree of certainty, simply based upon the way he holds his body and his sword. This concept is closely tied to the admonition against tarrying in a stance, since doing so makes the swordsman a ready mark. Japanese schools, too, espouse the belief that the respective postures of the swordsman and his opponent delimit the techniques that can be applied in a given encounter. This idea is often dramatized in the duels in samurai movies, in which the combatants circle one another, shifting from posture to posture.

Liechtenauer's verses advise the swordsman to use only four stances: *ochs* (ox), *pflug* (plow), *alber* (fool), and *vom dach* (from the roof). Each of these stances has a left and right side variation. Of these, the right side versions were considered the most important. Despite Liechtenauer's admonition to use only four stances, later masters developed a vast number of other positions. They justified this by classifying them as variations of the original four stances.

1) *Ochs* (ox): The ochs is a high stance, best suited for delivering attacks from above. In this stance, the swordsman holds the weapon next to his head, with the point sloping down toward his opponent. This drooping blade position gives the stance its name, since it resembles the lowered horns of an ox. This stance appears in various kenjutsu ryuha; for example, Shinkage-ryu calls this stance *jokaku jun*.[1]

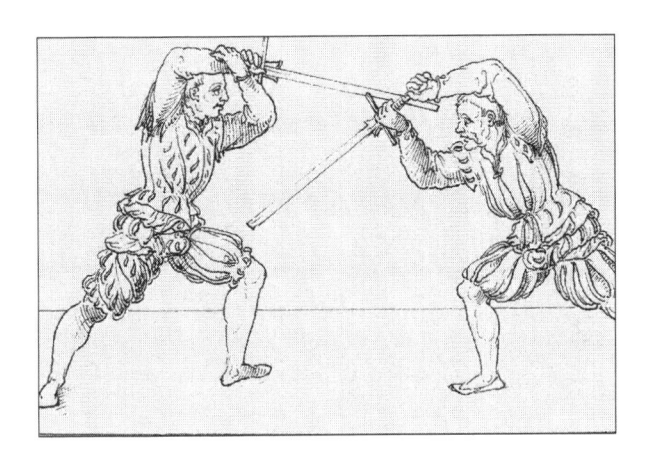

The right and left *ochs* (ox) stance, from a manual dating to around 1545. The blade positions are identical to those used in the *obere ansetzen*, the thrusts from above. Both swordsman use blunt-edged, flat-tipped practice swords.

The two Japanese stances are quite similar to the German *ochs* stance. Taken from a 17th century version of the *Heiho Kadensho*.

2) *Pflug* (plow): The *pflug* is a low stance which places the swordsman in an ideal position to cut or thrust upward at his opponent. The resulting pose roughly approximates the position taken when walking behind a plow, giving the stance its name. This stance appears in some Japanese schools as a variation of *chudan no kamae*.

A) The left and right *pflug* (plow) stance. The wrists of the right-hand swordsman are crossed, although the illustration obscures this fact. These two blade positions are identical to those used in the *untere ansetzen*, the thrusts from below.

B) *Chudan no kamae*, similar in some respects to the left plug stance. Unlike the German version, the Japanese stance has the arms extended forward, away from the body.

3) *Alber* (fool): This is a low stance which places the swordsman in an optimum position for defense. This stance takes its name from Liechtenauer's belief that only a fool stays on the defensive, relinquishing the initiative to his opponent. However, he acknowledged the superior defensive qualities of this stance by including it among his four. Other masters agreed, judging by another name for this stance—the *eiserne pforte* (iron gate). The *alber* stance is identical to the *gedan no kamae* found in many Japanese schools.

The swordsman on the left is in the *alber* (fool) stance. His opponent assumes the *vom dachf* (from the roof) stance. These positions are similar to the *gedan* and *jodan no kamae* commonly used in Japanese schools.

4) *Vom Dach* (from the roof): Like the *ochs*, this is a high stance, best suited for delivering cuts and thrusts from above. *Vom dach* is identical to the *jodan* stance used in most Japanese schools.

The German and Japanese systems share other stances as well. For example, the German school contains stances identical to the Japanese *wakigamae* and *basso no kamae*, to name but a few. The similarity between the two systems is more pronounced in the stances than in any other area. This is due in large part to simple body mechanics. Given a two-handed weapon, there are a limited number of positions in which the sword can be held.

Offensive and Defensive Principles

The most important lesson that Liechtenauer taught his students was the concept of *vor* (before) and *nach* (after). By *vor*, he meant the offensive principle; by *nach*, the defensive principle. The importance he assigned to this lesson is reflected in the following verse:

> *Vor und nach*
> *die zway ding*
> *sind aller kunst*
> *ain urspring*
>
> Before and after
> these two things
> are to all skill
> a well-spring

Vor (before): According to Liechtenauer's teachings, a good swordsman always attacks first, seizing the initiative before his opponent has the chance. Whether this first attack hits or misses is irrelevant, since it forces the opponent to parry the blow. Regardless of the outcome of his first strike, the swordsman keeps attacking, showering blows on his opponent. This keeps the enemy on the defensive, merely reacting to the rain of attacks. Ideally, the opponent is kept so busy defending himself that he cannot launch any attacks of his own. Any pause in this onslaught is a cardinal error, since it grants the opponent an opportunity to seize the initiative and go on the offensive.

The swordsman should vary his attacks—cutting, thrusting, striking with the pommel of the sword, even closing in to wrestle with the opponent. Furthermore, a good swordsman varies his targets, sometimes striking high, other times low, sometimes to the left, sometimes to the right. This variety confuses the opponent and keeps him off balance, so that he never knows where the next attack will come from.

Nach (After): If the opponent attacks first, the swordsman is left with the nach, or defensive principle. Liechtenauer taught that a swordsman who accepts this turn of events passively and merely parries his opponent's blows will eventually be struck and defeated. On the contrary, a good swordsman seeks to turn the tide by somehow regaining the initiative and going on the offensive.

The preferred method of regaining the initiative is by means of a counterattack. Ideally, the swordsman strikes in such a way that his sword deflects the incoming blow and hits the opponent at the same time. The most prized techniques in Liechtenauer's repertoire, known as the *meisterhau* (master cuts), are largely designed to accomplish this goal. In the words of one master, "Beware of the parries, which only poor swordsmen use. And note: if your opponent cuts, you should cut, too; if he thrusts, you should thrust, too."[16]

Attack and defense in one: although the swordsman on the left attacks first, his opponent steals the initiative from him by counterattacking with a cut underneath his blade. This cut will simultaneously parry the incoming blow and strike the opponent.

Another method of regaining the initiative is for the swordsman to parry the incoming attack. The parry is always combined with a sidestep, which diminishes the power of the attack and robs the attacker of his proper distance. After parrying, the swordsman immediately replies with an attack of his own before the opponent can strike again. However, since the attacker is already in motion, the German masters believed that it is easier for him to renew his attack than for the defender to riposte. Thus, they discouraged the use of parries, although they recognized that at times a swordsman has no choice.

In Japan, many kenjutsu schools use the concepts of *sen* (initiative) and *go* (response) to express similar ideas. *Sen* means to move before the opponent does, while *go* means allowing the enemy to move first. In addition to these relatively simple tactical concepts, some ryuha make use of more elaborate psychological constructs to analyze combat strategy. One example of this is the Shinkage family of ryuha, which place great importance on the concepts of *setsunin-to* (killing sword) and *katsujin-ken* (life-giving sword). In techniques applying *setsunin-to*, the swordsman psychologically dominates and cows his opponent. The swordsman who uses *katsujin-ken*, on the other hand, lulls his opponent into a false sense of security, using his overconfidence as a tool to defeat him. In the schools descended from the Shinkage-ryu, the latter was considered far superior to the former.[17]

Both the tactical concepts and combat psychology of the Japanese schools overlap to some degree with the German principles of *vor* and *nach*. The concept of *vor*, with its emphasis on striking first and dominating the opponent with incessant attacks, shares elements of both *sen* and *setsunin-to*. Despite the heavy bias against the *nach*, or defensive principle, the German manuals list certain techniques in which the swordsman deliberately exposes himself, inviting his opponent to attack. These techniques are similar to Japanese methods using both the concepts of *go* and *katsujin-ken*.

As opposed to the German school, with its pronounced bias in favor of the offensive, the Japanese schools hold varying opinions of the relative merit of attack and defense. Some schools prefer to wait for the opponent to attack. Others agree with Liechtenauer, instructing their students to attack first. Similarly, some schools see killing the opponent—even at the cost of one's own life—as the principal goal. Others see self-defense—even if the opponent escapes unscathed—as the true object of swordsmanship.

The Use of Leverage

The German masters divided the blade of the sword into two parts, known as the *stark* (strong) and the *schwech* (weak). The stark is the portion which reaches from the hilt up to the mid-point of the blade. Since this part of the blade is closest to the hands, it has the greatest leverage. Thus, the stark is the defensive part of the sword, used for parrying an opponent's blows. The schwech is the remainder of the blade, extending from the mid-section to the point of the sword. Since it is farthest from the hands, this part of the blade has the least amount of leverage. The schwech is the offensive part of the blade, used for cutting and thrusting.

Whenever the blades cross, each combatant typically seeks to press his stark against the *schwech* of the opposing sword. By applying superior leverage, the swordsman gains control of his adversary's sword and clears an opening for attack.

Mastery of this skill—the proper application of leverage—is extremely important in close combat, where the swords often come into contact.

In Japanese theory, the blade is usually divided into three parts: the *monouchi* (tip), the *chu-o* (middle) and the *tsuba moto* (closest to the guard). As in the German system, the monouchi is the offensive portion of the blade, while the tsuba moto is used to parry. In counterattacks, where the opponent's blade is deflected by the swordsman's cut, the *chu-o* is sometimes used to contact the opposing blade.

Although most Japanese schools tend to avoid the prolonged blade contact found in the German art, one ryu in particular specializes in techniques made with the swords crossed. Maniwa Nen-ryu places great emphasis on the proper use of leverage, training its students intensively in the engaged position known as *tsuba zerai*.[18]

Half-Sword
After parrying his opponent's thrust, the swordsman repostes with a pommel strike.

Gauging the Opponent's Blade Pressure

Whenever a swordsman contacts his opponent's blade—with a cut, a thrust, a parry, or by simply crossing the opposing sword—he should immediately determine whether the pressure against his blade is *hart* (hard) or *weich* (soft). Hard pressure is when the opponent presses his sword forcefully against the opposing blade. Soft pressure is when the opponent places minimal pressure on the blade. This blade pressure plays a key role in determining which technique the swordsman would use next.

Liechtenauer taught that a good swordsman opposes weakness with strength, and strength with weakness. If an opponent's blade pressure is soft, the swordsman opposes this weakness with strength: remaining in contact with the blade, he applies the proper leverage to force it aside, attacking on the same side that his blade is already on. On the other hand, if the opponent's blade pressure is hard, pressing forcefully against the swordsman's blade, he opposes this strength with weakness: suddenly giving way, he releases his opponent's blade and cuts around to the other side.

According to the German manuals, the ability to properly gauge the opponent's blade pressure is the greatest skill in swordsmanship. If a swordsman correctly gauges the blade pressure and makes an appropriate response, the opponent will be struck before he is aware of what has happened. The 'soft' opponent will find his blade forced aside, without the leverage or distance required to parry the incoming attack. The 'hard' opponent will find his blade travelling swiftly in the wrong direction, away from the incoming cut or thrust that he needs to parry. The harder he presses, the further his blade moves when the pressure is released, and the more he exposes himself on the other side.

Some Japanese schools contain teachings which use a hard/soft dichotomy similar to that found in the German system. For example, Araki-ryu teaches its students *in-yo gaku*, the interplay of yin and yang. However, this school gives the hard/soft concept a much wider scope, applying it not only to physical technique, but also to tactical approaches and combat psychology.[19] Although other ryuha may lack an explicit expression of the concepts mentioned above, an understanding of these principles is implicit in many of their kata. Maniwa Nen-ryu, in particular, employs techniques in which the swordsman either forces his way through a weak engagement, or releases his opponent's hard pressure, cutting around to the other side. However, Japanese swordsmanship on the whole tends to avoid prolonged blade contact. As a result, these concepts are usually less important in the Japanese ryuha than they are in the German system.

Zufechten—The First Phase of Combat

The German masters divided combat into two phases. The *zufechten* is the initial phase, in which the swordsman closes distance with his opponent. Starting out of striking distance, the swordsman assumes a stance and approaches his adversary. Stepping swiftly toward his opponent, the swordsman makes his first attack, usually a cut.

This first attack is usually made from the right side. When cutting from the right side, a swordsman's arms are uncrossed. Cuts from the left require him to cross his right wrist over the left. This latter position, with the wrists crossed, is weak, awkward, and unnatural. This is especially the case once the swords cross, and the application of leverage becomes important. As a result, the German masters preferred cuts made with the arms *offen* (open) as opposed to those in which the wrists are *krump* (crooked or twisted).

An inexperienced swordsman often fixates on his opponent's weapon, since it poses a threat to him. In the initial phase of combat, the novice often attempts to close distance by cutting at the opposing blade, seeking to beat it aside. Liechtenauer considered this a grave error. He believed that every action a swordsman makes should threaten the opponent, forcing him to parry unless he wants to be hit. In this way, the swordsman keeps the initiative and dictates his opponent's moves. Since the act of beating the blade aside poses no danger to the opponent, he is free to simply evade the attempt to strike his blade, taking the opportunity to attack. Thus, cutting at the opponent's sword instead of his body amounts to a voluntary relinquishment of the initiative—a cardinal sin in Liechtenauer's eyes. As one early master said, a good swordsman ". . . should act as if his opponent has no sword, or as if he doesn't see it. . . ."[20] Conversely, a swordsman should be skilled at evading the opponent's sword whenever he attempts to make contact, seizing the initiative and attacking the momentary opening that results.

Also belonging to the zufechten phase are a variety of feints. Two primary methods are used. In the first, the swordsman simply pulls his blow before it lands, and then cuts or thrusts at another target. In the second method, the swordsman intentionally misses his opponent, cutting past him into another stance. From this new position, he makes his final attack at another opening. In both types, the feint begins as a real attack; the swordsman only evades the opposing blade when it appears likely that the opponent will parry the blow.

The concept of closing distance is central to most Japanese ryuha. They typically identify three types of encounters, based on the initial distance between the combatants: *yukiai* (going encounter), in which the combatants begin well out of range; *tachiai* (standing encounter), in which the combatants begin just out of range, with the sword tips barely crossed; and *iai* (seated encounter) in which one or more of the combatants is seated or kneeling. Mastery of the subtleties of *maai*, or combat distance, is considered especially important when using the sword against an unequal weapon—whether it be a tanto, yari, or naginata.

Although the Japanese schools lack an explicit teaching on the subject, their kata make clear that they share the German preference for making the first attack from the right. Cuts from the left, with the wrists crossed, are widely regarded as comparatively weak and awkward, and are generally avoided.

Krieg—The Second Phase of Combat

The realities of combat are such that a swordsman's initial attack is rarely successful. As a result, the combatants often find themselves facing each other at arms length, behind crossed swords. The manuals call this second phase of combat the *krieg* (war), also known as *handarbeit* (hand-work). In this phase, the swordsman fight at close range, exchanging cuts, thrusts, and parries.[21]

During the krieg phase, the swordsman showers his opponent with attacks. As soon as one is parried, he begins another. Since the blades are in such frequent contact, the swordsman must continually gauge his opponent's blade pressure, responding appropriately with 'soft' or 'hard' techniques. Meanwhile, the defending swordsman attempts to somehow regain the initiative, forcing the attacker onto the defensive.

Liechtenauer taught that whenever the blades cross, three main types of attack are possible: a thrust, a cut, and a *schnitt* (slice), a slicing or drawing cut. These three options are known as the *drey wunder* (ghree wounders). Knowing which of the three to use is an important skill in close combat. In large part, this choice is based on the swordsman's distance from his adversary: the thrust is a long range attack, the cut is used at medium range, and the *schnitt* is most effective at close range. Choosing the wrong option is a potentially fatal mistake, since the swordsman must adjust his distance to compensate—losing valuable time in the process.

The techniques allocated to the *krieg* phase can be broken down into two types. The first group of techniques, *vom schwert* (from the sword), are made by leaving the opponent's blade. For example, if the opponent parries his cut, the swordsman removes his sword from contact with the opposing blade, striking at another opening. This new attack can be made as a cut, thrust, *schnitt* (drawing cut), or even by striking with the pommel of the sword. These techniques are made with an absence of blade contact, aside from incidental contact resulting from an adversary's belated parry.

The second group of techniques are made *am schwert* (on the sword). These are attacks made without leaving the opposing blade, maintaining constant blade contact throughout the course of the attack. Better known as the *winden* (winding or turning), these techniques are one of the hallmarks of the *kunst des fechtens*. They typically involve the application of superior leverage against the opponent's blade. Pressing the *stark* (strong) of his blade against the opponent's *schwech* (weak), the swordsman clears an opening, while simultaneously sliding along the opposing blade to strike his head or torso. The name is derived from the winding, turning motion of the sword along its axis.

The *winden* have two main advantages. First is the control they allow over the opposing blade, since the swordsman's blade never leaves his opponent's. Second is their speed, since the blade is already close to the opponent when the attack begins. Their only disadvantage is their relative lack of force. Although these *zecken* or 'taps' with the sword are comparatively light, they often catch the opponent by surprise. This, in turn, often triggers an overreaction by the flustered opponent as he belatedly attempts to parry, creating an opportunity for the swordsman to deliver a killing blow to another target.

A similar division of combat into phases is found in Shinkage-ryu. According to a commentary on the *Heiho Kadensho*, the term *jo* refers to the period before the attack, *ha* to the initial attack, and *kyu* to the exchanging of blows that occurs after the first attack.[22] Thus, *jo* and *ha* correspond to the German *zufechten*, while *kyu* seems to be the same as the *krieg* or *handarbeit* phase of combat.

Although both systems divide combat into similar phases, the methods used once the blades cross vary greatly. Techniques such as the *winden*—cutting or thrusting without leaving the opponent's blade—appear with much less frequency in the Japanese schools. Although some schools, such as Maniwa Nen-ryu, do use these techniques, the general Japanese tendency is to avoid prolonged blade contact. One reason for this may be the length of the blades; since the German sword is longer, the swordsman are farther apart when the blades are crossed. This greater distance translates into greater reaction time for the swordsman. In comparison, the shorter Japanese blade places the combatants at much closer range when the blades are crossed. The swordsman are so close that they have much less time to react, making this engaged position far more dangerous.

A *winden*, an attack made while maintaining blade contact. The left-hand swordsman's initial attack, a *scheitelhau* (vertical downward cut), has been parried. Remaining in contact with the opposing blade, he hooks over his opponent's parry with a back-edge cut to the head. This illustration comes from Albrecht Duerer's manual of 1512.

Another *winden*, from Hans Talhoffer's manual of 1467. Originally, both swordsman were in the position assumed by the man on the left. The right-hand swordsman, sensing hard pressure on the blade, steps in with a thrust at his opponent. By uncrossing his arms, he can reach around the opposing blade with a thrust. The opponent's hard pressure causes his blade to follow, and prevents him from simply thrusting forward at his attacker's belly.

Half-Sword Techniques

Another hallmark of the German school is a series of techniques in which the swordsman grasps the blade of the sword in his left hand, while holding the grip in his right. Holding the sword in this fashion, the swordsman uses it like a short spear to thrust at his opponent. The German masters referred to these as *halb-schwert* (half-sword) techniques. Designed primarily for use in armored combat, these methods were deemed so effective that many swordsman used them even when fighting unarmored. Although grasping a sharp blade would seem to create a risk of injury, the swordsman's hand was usually protected by a leather glove. These techniques were perfected by Master Martin Hundsfeld and Master Andre Liegnitzer, whose writings on the subject were widely copied.[23]

These half-sword techniques include ready stances, thrusts, pommel strikes, and parries—all with the left hand gripping the blade, Other moves include hooking and trapping maneuvers using the point, the pommel, or the cross hilt. With slight adjustments for the length of the weapon, these methods could easily be adapted for use with a spear or lance.

One of the most common half-sword techniques is the *kron* (crown) parry, used against a vertical downwards cut to the head. Holding the sword over his head with the point forward, the swordsman catches the incoming cut on the portion of the blade between his hands. This parry is typically followed by a thrust over the opponent's right arm at his face. In a more sophisticated version of this, the parry and thrust can be made as a single move, simultaneously blocking and striking the opponent.

Two half-sword stances, from Hans Talhoffer's manual of 1467. The swordsman on the left prepares to thrust from above; his opponent, from below.

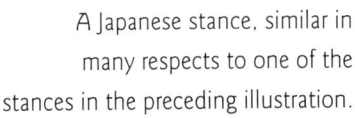

A Japanese stance, similar in many respects to one of the stances in the preceding illustration.

Half-sword techniques appear in some Japanese schools as well. Although most kenjutsu ryuha tend to avoid these methods, a few schools seem to specialize in them. Katori Shinto-ryu, in particular, contains a large number of these techniques in its kata.[24] For example, the *kron* parry mentioned above is nearly identical to the *tori* (temple gate) parry of this school. Other techniques involve cuts, thrusts and parries in which the blade is supported by the left hand. When using half-sword techniques, the Japanese swordsman typically pinches the blade between his thumb and forefinger, or rests the blunt back edge on the palm of his hand.

The main difference between the German and Japanese systems in this respect is the importance they ascribe to the techniques. In the Japanese system, these techniques are fairly uncommon, and appear to be a late development. Thus, they appear with greater frequency in the more recent iaido schools than they do in the older kenjutsu ryuha, with the exception of Katori Shinto-ryu. In contrast, half-sword techniques were a specialty of the German masters. In some of the surviving manuals, they comprise the majority of the repertoire. So common were these methods that artists depicted the German emperor himself using them on more than one occasion.[25]

The swordsman on the left parries a downwards cut by sidestepping, hooking behind his opponent's blade, and guiding the cut past him. This type of redirecting parry was used against a strong opponent; against a weaker adversary, the swordsman would receive the cut on the portion of the blade between his hands.

A similar Japanese parry, supporting the blade on the palm of the left hand. This type of parry is called *tori* (temple gate) by the Katori Shinto-ryu. After receiving his opponent's cut, the swordsman thrusts over the opponent's arm at his face.

The greater popularity of these techniques in Germany is most likely due to the longer blade of the German sword. At close range, a technique that suddenly shortens the effective length of such a long blade is especially effective. In addition to allowing thrusts at extremely close range, these techniques give the swordsman much greater leverage than an opponent who uses a more conventional grip on the sword. In comparison, the Japanese blade is so short that only minimal advantage is gained by using such techniques.

Conclusion

In retrospect, it should not be surprising that two societies, each with a professional warrior class, should develop similar approaches to the martial arts. Considering the highly efficient armor used in both cultures, the focus on a two-handed weapon is also understandable. Given the mechanics of the human body, the similarity in ready stances and other basic elements of technique is only natural. The differences in technique which do exist are readily explained by the characteristics of the weapon itself, such as the length of blade or the number of edges.

Of course, certain aspects of both systems of swordsmanship are the result of cultural factors. For example, the emphasis on kata as a teaching method can be seen as part of a larger trend throughout all of the Japanese arts. Likewise, the spiritual emphasis so apparent in the Japanese martial tradition stems from the importance of esoteric forms of Buddhism, and later Zen, to the warrior class. Neither of these cultural factors existed in medieval Germany; thus, these elements are lacking in the Kunst des Fechtens. The German system, in turn, was influenced by larger intellectual currents in Europe. The first of the manuals, written by a German priest, even quotes Aristotle to support one of Liechtenauer's principles.[26] This close connection to the major sources of Western thought is reflected in the standard methodology used by German masters: beginning with general principles, they proceed to specific examples.

Finally, despite the misconceptions so rampant in the field, even a cursory study of the German manuals reveals a system of martial arts that was sophisticated, systematic, and highly effective. Far from an unskilled ruffian who relied on strength alone, the medieval knight is revealed in his true colors: a skilled professional, expert in his weapons, and possessed of a deadly repertoire of techniques—as effective, in every significant respect, as his counterparts in feudal Japan.

Acknowledgements for Source Material

The comparative portions of this chapter are based on extensive correspondence and interviews with various kenjutsu instructors and practitioners. Foremost among these were Kim Taylor, Karl Friday, and Ellis Amdur. I remain indebted to a host of others, far too numerous to mention by name.

APPENDIX
The Primary Techniques with the Long Sword

Master Liechtenauer's verses list seventeen *hauptstuecke* (primary techniques) used in unarmored combat with the long sword. First come the five *meisterhau* (master cuts), a series of especially effective cuts made with the sword. They are followed by the remaining twelve techniques which Master Liechtenauer considered most useful in combat.

1) *Zornhau* (**rage cut**): A diagonal downwards cut which deflects the opponent's attack, while simultaneously striking him in the face with the point. This cut derives its name from Liechtenauer's recognition that a swordsman striking in anger will instinctively use this cut, which is a downward diagonal cut from the right shoulder.
2) *Krumphau* (**crooked cut**): A downwards cut, made with the back edge of the blade, which strikes the opponent's wrist. This technique is usually made while sidestepping to avoid the opponent's attack; the blow strikes the opponent's wrist, stopping his attack. The name is based on the *"krump"* (crooked or twisted) position of the swordsman's wrists, which are crossed in the process of making the blow.
3) *Zwerchhau* (**cross cut**): A horizontal cut which simultaneously deflects the opponent's attack and strikes him on the side of the head. The name derives from the horizontal trajectory of the blow.
4) *Schielhau* (**squinting cut**): A downwards cut, made with the back edge of the blade, which simultaneously deflects the opponent's attack and strikes him on the shoulder or neck. This cut is made with a pivoting sidestep. In the final position, the swordsman can only see his opponent out of one eye; hence the name.
5) *Schaitelhau* (**scalp cut**): A vertical downwards cut at the opponent's head, made with the very tip of the blade. The name is derived from the target of the attack.
6) *Vier Leger* (**four stances**): Described in the main body of this article, these are the *ochs* (ox), *pflug* (plow), *alber* (fool), and *vom dach* (from the roof).
7) *Vier Versetzen* (**four counters**): These are specific methods for attacking each of the four stances mentioned above. This series of verses also contains methods for dealing with an opponent who parries the swordsman's attack. The name comes from the spe-

cialized attacks which counter the defensive advantages of particular stances.

8) ***Nachraissen* (attacking after):** Methods for regaining the initiative, should the opponent manage to attack first. These include dodging the opponent's attack, striking him while he is in the midst of his attack, and other methods. The name refers to the timing of the technique, since the swordsman allows his opponent to attack first before beginning his own "*raissen*" or attack.

9) ***Ueberlauffen* (overrunning):** If the opponent strikes at the lower parts of the body, the swordsman is instructed to ignore the attack, instead striking at the upper parts of his adversary's body. Thus, he out reaches the opponent's attack.

10) ***Absetzen* (setting aside):** Methods for parrying the opponent's cuts and thrusts. The emphasis is on parries which simultaneously deflect the incoming attack and strike the opponent. The name is based on the motion with which the opponent's incoming attack is deflected.

11) ***Durchwechseln* (changing through):** Techniques for evading the opponent's blade, used when the opponent attempts to parry the swordsman's attack. Also used when the opponent attempts to beat the swordsman's point aside. The name derives from the way in which the swordsman changes the direction of his attack by passing underneath his opponent's blade. This is similar to the modern fencer's disengagement.

12) ***Zucken* (pulling around):** Repetitive, side-to-side cutting in response to the opponent's attempts to parry. The name refers to motion with which the sword is pulled or swung around the swordsman's head while striking to the other side.

13) ***Durchlauffen* (running through):** Grappling and throwing techniques used at close quarters. The technique takes its name from the way in which the swordsman ducks and "runs through" under the opponent's arms as he closes to grappling distance.

14) ***Abschneiden* (slicing down):** Drawing cuts, made with a slicing motion against one or both of the opponent's arms. Occasionally, drawing cuts were used against the opponent's face as well. These are divided into *ober schnitt* (made with a downwards motion) and *unter schnitt* (made in an upwards direction).

15) ***Hende Trucken* (pressing the hands):** Similar to *abschneiden*, this series of techniques involves striking the opponent's hands as he attacks.

16) ***Zwai Hengen* (two hangers):** These are the primary positions formed when the blades cross. This series of techniques deals with the tactical approaches which are most useful in this situation. The name is derived from the way in which the sword blade hangs downwards toward the ground in some of the positions discussed.

17) ***Acht Winden* (eight windings):** A specialized series of attacks used when the swords are crossed. These techniques are made without ever losing contact with the opponent's blade. They allow the swordsman to retain control of the opposing sword, while simultaneously reaching around it to deliver the attack. The name is based on the winding, turning motion of the sword along its axis.

Footnotes

1. No biographical data exists for Johannes Liechtenauer. The sole source of information concerning his life are the manuals written by the masters who followed in his footsteps. Liechtenauer was most likely born in the early or mid-14th century. Judging from clues in the text of the earliest manual, he may have been alive when it was written in 1389.
2. For example, the writings of Master Ott appear in the manuals of Hans Talhoffer (1443) and Jud Lew (n.d.); the writings of Master Leckuechner appear in Christian Egenolph's printed work (misspelled as "Lebkommer") and Albrecht Duerer's manual (1512).
3. A manuscript dating from 1579 at the German National Museum in Nuremberg contains a series of rhymes by members of the Marxbrueder and a rival organization, the Federfechter. Among the Marxbrueder are candlemakers, furriers, and potters; the Federfechter are goldsmiths, knifesmiths, and shoemakers. The origins of the individuals mentioned in this manuscript show how widespread the art had become by the late 16th century: Munich in Bavaria, Hof in Austria, Breslau in Silesia, Lubeck and Danzig on the Baltic coast, Dresden in Saxony. This manuscript is reproduced in the works of both Alfred Schaer (1901) and Karl Wassmansdorff (1870).
4. Pauernfeindt, 1516.
5. Draeger, 1973a:70.
6. Meyer, 1570:2 recto.
7. Still, as late as 1725, the Shogun Yoshimune imported the German riding instructor, Hans Jurgen Keyserling, to teach his courtiers the Western style of riding and fighting on horseback. This not only shows that some Germans made the journey east, but that they engaged in technical instruction as well. Keyserling's story appears in Hesselink (1995). Furthermore, a series of prints by the Dutch swordsman Martin Heemskerk in 1552 make clear that the German long sword style was practiced in the Netherlands. Conceivably, Dutch swordsmen could have carried German long sword techniques with them to Japan.
8. This quote appears in the 10th century *Chanson de Geste of Girart de Roussillon*.
9. For an excellent discussion of the development of European armor, see *Edge and Paddock* (1988).
10. The Metropolitan Museum of Art in New York has in its collection a matched set of practice swords of a type illustrated in many of the German manuals. The statistics for these two swords follow: overall length = 50.6"; blade length = 40.75"; weight = 2 pounds, 14 ounces.

11. The most widely used typology for medieval European swords is that developed by R. Ewart Oakeshott (1964). The long swords pictured in the various German manuals fall into types XIIIa, XVa, XVIa, XVII, XVIIIb, XVIIIe, and XX in Mr. Oakeshott's typology. This includes nearly all of the weapons classified variously as "war swords" or "hand-and-a-half swords."
12. Doebringer, 1389:23 verso, 24 recto.
13. Wilhalm, 1523:3 verso. Joerg Wilhalm produced five manuals, all of which were nearly identical.
14. See, for example, the katas depicted in Watanabe (1993). Nearly all of the attacks are downward cuts directed at the upper body and arms.
15. Ibid., Volume 1, page 12.
16. Ringeck, 1440's:35 recto.
17. Personal communication from Dr. Karl F. Friday, who holds the rank of shihan/menkyo kaiden in the Kashima Shin-ryu, a comprehensive system of battlefield martial arts which traces its origins to the 15th century.
18. See the discussion of "dynamic tension" in Amdur (1995).
19. Personal communication from Mr. Ellis Amdur, M.A. Mr. Amdur is an instructor (*shihan-dai*) in Araki-ryu Torite Kogusoku, and a master instructor (*shihan*) in Tada-ha Buko-ryu Naginatajutsu.
20. Doebringer, 1389: 19 verso.
21. Later manuals also describe a third phase, *abziehen* (retreat), but this concept is not representative of the school as a whole.
22. Sato, 1985: 52, note 1.
23. For example, the writings of these two masters appear in the manuals of Peter von Danzig (1452) and Jud Lew (n.d.).
24. See the katas depicted in Otake (1978).
25. See, for example, the *Great and Small Armorials of the Order of the Golden Fleece* at the Bibliotheque Nacionale and the Bibliotheque de l'Arsenal in Paris, which date from the 1430's or 1440's.
26. Doebringer, 1389:22 verso.

Bibliography of German Fencing Manuals

Below are listed some of the more important manuals connected with Liechtenauer's school, arranged roughly in chronological order.

Doebringer, Hanko. (1389). *Fechtbuch*. n.p. Codex Ms. 3227a at the German National Museum in Nuremberg. This is the earliest work containing the verses of Johannes Liechtenauer.

Ringeck, Sigmund. (n.d.). *Fechtbuch*. n.p. Mscr. Dresd. C 487, State Library of

Saxony, Dresden, Germany. This important work dates to some time in the 1440's.

Talhoffer, Hans. (1443). *Fechtbuch*. n.p. (Gotha Codex); Ms. Chart. A 558, Research Library at Schloss Friedenstein, Gotha, Germany. This work was the first of many published by Talhoffer.

Anonymous. (n.d.). *Fechtbuch*. n.p. Codex I.6.4o.2, Central Library of the University of Augsburg. This book contains at least two 15th century works which were later bound together.

von Danzig, Peter. (1452). *Fechtbuch*. n.p. Codex 44 A 8 at the Library of the National Academy (Lincei e Corsiniana) in Rome, Italy.

Lew, Jud. (n.d.). *Fechtbuch*. n.p. Codex I.6.4o.3, Central Library of the University of Augsburg. This important work dates from around 1450–1460.

Kal, Paulus. (n.d.). *Fechtbuch*. n.p. Codex Germanicus 1507 at the State Library of Bavaria in Munich, Germany. This manual dates from around 1460–1470.

Talhoffer, Hans. (1467). *Fechtbuch*. n.p. (Munich Codex); Codex Icon. 394a at the State Library of Bavaria in Munich, Germany. This work was the last of Talhoffer's manuals.

Leckuechner, Johannes. (1482). *Fechtbuch*. n.p. Codex Germanicus 582 at the State Library of Bavaria in Munich, Germany.

von Speyer, H. (1491). *Fechtbuch*. n.p. M. I. 29, located at the Library of the University of Salzburg in Salzburg, Austria.

Falkner, Peter. (n.d.). *Fechtbuch*. n.p. Manuscript P 5012 at the Art History Museum in Vienna, Austria. A *hauptmann* (captain) of the Marxbrueder, Falkner's manual appears to date from the 1490's.

Duerer, Albrecht. (1512). *Fechtbuch*. n.p. Manuscript 26–232 at the Graphics Collection at the Albertina Museum, Vienna, Austria. Albrecht Duerer was the most important artist of the Renaissance in Northern Europe. Although Duerer was not a fencing master himself, he appears to have been intimately familiar with the art.

Pauernfeindt, Andre. (1516). *Fechtbuch* (*Ergrundung ritterlicher kunst der fechterey*). Vienna, Austria: n.p. This was later re-published in French under the title *La noble science des joueurs d'espee*, Antwerp, 1538.

Wilhalm, Joerg. (1522–23). *Fechtbuch*. n.p. Codex Germanicus 3711 at the State Library of Bavaria in Munich, Germany.

Wilhalm, Joerg. (1523). *Fechtbuch*. n.p. I.6.2o.2. Located at the Central Library of the University of Augsburg.

Egenolff, Christian. (1531). *Fechtbuch* (*Der altenn fechter an fengliche kunst . . .*). Frankfurt am Main: n.p. This manual appeared in many editions from 1531 to 1558. Many copies of this work exist at libraries throughout Europe and the

United States.

Erhart, Gregor. (1533). *Augsburg's fechtbuch*. n.p. Formerly Codex I.6.4o.4 at the Library of the University of Augsburg. Until recently thought to be lost, it was recently discovered by Professor Sydney Anglo at the Scott Collection in Glasgow, Scotland.

Mair, Paulus Hector. (n.d.). *Fechtbuch*. n.p. Mscr. Dresd. C 93/94, State Library of Saxony, Dresden, Germany. This work dates from around 1550. It is a monumental, two-volume compendium, over 1,000 pages long. Mair produced two other compendia which are nearly as long.

Anonymous. (1539). *Fechtbuch*. n.p. Probably written by a student of Hans Niedel of Salzburg; Cod. I.6.2o.5, located at the Library of the University of Augsburg in Augsburg, Germany.

Meyer, Joachim. (1570). *Grundtliche beschreibung der freyen ritterlichen und adelichen kunst des fechtens* (Basic Description of the Free, Knightly, and Noble Art of Fighting). Strasbourg (Alsace): n.p. A second edition was published in Augsburg in 1600. This important work can be found in many libraries in Europe and the United States.

Sutor, Jakob. (1612). *Fechtbuch (New kuenstliches fechtbuch)*. Frankfurt am Main: n.p. This late work devotes more space to the rapier than it does to the long sword.

Works Describing the German Fencing Manuals

Edge, David, and Paddock, John. (1988). *Arms and armor of the medieval knight*. New York: Crescent Books.

Hergsell, Gustav. (1896). *Die fechtkunst im 15 und 16 jahrhundert*. Prague: n.p.

Hils, Hans-Peter. (1985). Meister Johann Liechtenauers kunst des langen schwerts. *Europaische Hochschulschriften*, Vol. 257. Frankfurt am Main: Peter Lang.

Lochner, Karl Ernst. (1953). *Die entwicklungsphasen der europaischen fechtkunst*. Vienna: n.p.

Oakeshott, R. Ewart. (1964). *The sword and the age of chivalry*. Woodbridge, UK: Boydell Press.

Schaer, Alfred. (1901). *Die altdeutschen fechter und spielleute*. Strasbourg: n.p.

Wassmannsdorff, Alfred. (1870). *Sechs fechtschulen der Marxbrueder und Federfechter aus den jahren 1573 bis 1614*. Heidelberg: n.p.

Wierschin, Martin. (1965). *Meister Johann Liechtenauers kunst des fechtens*. Munich: Muenchener Texte und Untersuchungen zur deutschen Literatur des Mittelalters.

Works on the Japanese Sword Arts

Amdur, Ellis. (1995). Maniwa Nen-ryu. *Journal of Asian Martial Arts*, 4: 3, 10–25.

Draeger, Donn F. (1973a). *Classical budo*. New York: Weatherhill.

Draeger, Donn F. (1973b). *Classical bujutsu*. New York: Weatherhill.

Harris, Victor. (1974). *A book of five rings*. Woodstock, NY: The Overlook Press.

Hesselink, Reinier H. (1995). The warrior's prayer–Tokugawa Yoshimune revives the yabusame ceremony. *Journal of Asian Martial Arts*, 4: 4, 40–49.

Otake, Ritsuke. (1978). *The deity and the sword* (Vols. 1–3). Tokyo: Minato Research and Publishing Co.

Sato, Hiroaki. (1986). *The sword and the mind*. Woodstock, NY: The Overlook Press.

Stevens, John. (1984). *The sword of no sword*. Boulder, CO: Shambhala Press.

Warner, Gordon, and Draeger, Donn F. (1982). *Japanese swordsmanship: Technique and practice*. New York: Weatherhill.

Watanabe, Tadashige. (1993). *Shinkage-ryu sword techniques* (Vols. I and II). Tokyo: Sugawara Martial Arts Institute, Inc.

index

aikido, 1, 41
Anatomical Tables (Anatomische Tabellen), 30
Araki-ryu, 63, 73 note 19
bakufu, 4, 17
Bodhidharma, 18
Bokuden, Tsukahara, 42
broadsword, 38
buckler, 50
Buddhism, 17, 19, 26, 69
budo, 10, 25, 27, 31
bugei, 6
bujutsu, 6, 10–11, 17, 25, 31
bushido, 7, 21, 27
Christianity, 3, 6, 26, 29
Confucianism, 7, 20–21, 28
d'Almeida, Louis, 29
Daoism, 19, 22, 43 note 2
Deshima Island, 29
Dogen, 20
Dutch, 29–31, 38, 48, 72 note 7
education of warriors, 4–6, 9, 16
Eisai, 20
five elements, 23-24
five human relationships, 7, 26
four cardinal humors, 29
geometry, 36–39, 42
German, 29–31, 45–71
Greek, 16, 29, 38
halbard, 49–50
hierarchical society, 2, 26
Hong Ren, 18
Iizasa Choisai Ienao, 47-48
intuition, 7, 21
Italian sword school, 39

Itto-ryu, 54
Jesuits, 26
jousts, 9
judo, 1, 16
jutsu, 6, 10, 17, 25
Kaitai Shinsho (New Text on Anatomy), 30
kami, 17–18, 22
Kamiizumi, Hidetsuna, 48
karate, 1, 16
Kashima Shrine, 48
katana, 52
kenjutsu, 46, 48, 53–54, 56–57, 61, 68, 70
Hanaoka, Seishu, 30
Heiho Kadensho, 57, 65
Hundsfeld, Martin, 67
Katori Shrine, 48
Katori Shinto-ryu, 47, 68
knight, defined, 3
Kulmus, Johann Adam, 30
Lecküchner, Hans, 47
legal contracts, 2
Liegnitzer, Andre, 67
Liechtenauer, Johannes, 46–48, 50, 53 55–57, 59–65, 69–70, 72 note 1, 73
Liechtenauer's four stances, 56–57, 70
Maeno, Ryotaku, 30
Maniwa Nen-ryu, 62, 63, 66
martial sport, 2, 4, 9–14, 39
Maurice of Nassau, 38
medicine, 9, 16, 23–24, 29–31
messer, 47, 50
Meyer, Joachim, 47–49, 51
Middle Ages, 2, 4, 6–8, 14–15, 17, 20–21, 26, 36
Minamoto, Yoritomo, 4, 17

Nagashino, Battle of, 48
Neo-Confucianism, 7, 20–21, 26–28
New Book for Understanding the Human Body, 30
Nobunaga, Oda, 48
Ott the Jew, 46–47, 72 note 2
philosophy, 4, 16, 37, 45, 48
poleaxe, 50
Portugal, 29, 48
prisoners, 8
purification, 15
Pythagoras, 37
ransom, 6, 8
rapier, 38, 40, 47–49, 54, 75
Renaissance, 4, 8, 36–39, 42, 43 note 6, 55
Ringeck, Sigmund, 46
Rinzai Zen School, 20
ritual suicide (seppuku/harakiri), 3, 6–7, 20–21
Roman, 3–5, 38–39
samurai, defined, 3
shield, 38, 50
Shinkage-ryu, 56–57, 61, 65

Shinto, 17, 20–22, 26
shogun, 4–5, 21, 23, 26, 29, 48, 72 note 7
Soto Zen School, 20
Spain, 38, 43 note 7
staff, 49–50
Sugita, Gempaku, 30
taijiquan, 1, 36
Taira Family, 4
Talhoffer, Hans, 46, 66–67, 72 note 2
Tokugawa, Ieyasu, 25
Tokugawa Period, 4, 7, 10, 21–24, 25–27, 29, 31, 48
tournaments, 8–10
vassal, 2–3, 7, 21
von Siebold, Philipp, 31
warrior code (bushido), 6–7, 18, 21, 23–24, 26–27, 45
women, conception of, 3, 8, 21
Xavier, Francis, 26
Yagyu Family, 48
Yagyu Shinkage-ryu, 56–57, 61, 65
Yamawaki, Toyo, 30
Zen, 3, 7, 17–23, 26–27, 69
Zhu Xi, 27–28

Printed in Great Britain
by Amazon